SHONEN JUMP

THE WORLD'S MOST POPULAR MANGA

STORY AND ART BY
TITE KUBO

STORY AND ART BY
EIICHIRO ODA

STORY AND ART BY
HIROYUKI ASADA

JUMP INTO THE ACTION BY TELLING US WHAT YOU LOVE (AND WHAT YOU DON'T)

LET YOUR VOICE BE HEARD!

SHONENJUMP.VIZ.COM/MANGASURVEY

HELP US MAKE MORE OF THE WORLD'S MOST POPULAR MANGA!

BLEACH © 2001 by Tite Kubo/SHUEISHA Inc.
ONE PIECE © 1997 by Eiichiro Oda/SHUEISHA Inc.
TEGAMIBACHI © 2006 by Hiroyuki Asada/SHUEISHA Inc.

RATED T FOR TEEN

SJ

A boy, a dragon, and one high-flying adventure of a lifetime!

DRAGON DRIVE™

Manga on sale now!

$7.99

DRAGON DRIVE 1
SHONEN JUMP MANGA
Story & Art by Ken-ichi Sakura
volume 1

SHONEN JUMP MANGA

DRAGON DRIVE © 2001 by Ken-ichi Sakura/SHUEISHA I

On sale at:
www.shonenjump.com
Also available at your local bookstore and comic store.

www.viz.com

SJ
Turn fantasy into REALity!
LEGENDZ
TALE OF THE DRAGON KINGS
BY RIN HIRAI

MANGA SERIES
ON SALE NOW
ONLY
$7.99

SHONEN JUMP
THE WORLD'S MOST POPULAR MANGA

On sale at: www.shonenjump.com
Also available at your local bookstore and comic store.

LEGENDZ © 2003 by Makoto Haruno, Rin Hirai/
SHUEISHA Inc. © 2003 WIZ

RATED
A
FOR
ALL AGES
ratings.viz.com

VIZ media
www.viz.com

CAN YUGI FIGHT HIS WAY TO THE TOP OF THE DUEL MONSTERS TOURNAMENT...AND EARN THE TITLE OF DUELIST KING?
SJ
MANGA ON SALE NOW!
YU-GI-OH! DUELIST
SHONEN JUMP GRAPHIC NOVEL
Story & Art by
Kazuki Takahashi volume 1
$7.95
YU-GI-OH! DUELIST™
SHONEN JUMP MANGA
On sale at:
www.shonenjump.com
Also available at your local bookstore and comic store.
RATED T FOR TEEN
VIZ media
www.viz.com
YU-GI-OH! © 1996 by Kazuki Takahashi/SHUEISHA Inc.

Princess Pig

by Molly Coxe

Kane Press • New York

For all bright-eyed, bright owl readers.

Copyright © 2018 by Molly Coxe

All rights reserved. No part of this book may be reproduced or transmitted in any form or by any means, electronic or mechanical, including photocopying, recording, or by any information storage and retrieval system, without permission in writing from the publisher. For information regarding permission, contact the publisher through its website: www.kanepress.com.
Originally published in different form by BraveMouse Books in 2014.
Copyright © 2014 Molly Coxe

Library of Congress Cataloging-in-Publication Data
Names: Coxe, Molly, author, illustrator.
Title: Princess pig / by Molly Coxe.
Description: First Kane Press edition. | New York : Kane Press, [2018] |
Series: Bright Owl Books | "Originally published in different form by BraveMouse Books in 2014"—Title page verso. | Summary: "Pig and Twig are playing princess, but even after Princess Pig has used her three wishes, she wants to make more"— Provided by publisher.
Identifiers: LCCN 2018007760 (print) | LCCN 2017038645 (ebook) | ISBN 9781575659800 (pbk) | ISBN 9781575659794 (pbk) | ISBN 9781575659787 (reinforced library binding) | ISBN 9781575659800 (ebook)
Subjects: | CYAC: Friendship—Fiction. | Pigs—Fiction. | Mice—Fiction. | Wishes—Fiction.
Classification: LCC PZ7.C839424 (print) | LCC PZ7.C839424 Pr 2018 (ebook) | DDC [E]—dc23
LC record available at https://lccn.loc.gov/2018007760

10 9 8 7 6 5 4 3 2 1

Printed in China

Book Design: Michelle Martinez

Bright Owl Books is a trademark of Kane Press, Inc.

Visit us online at www.kanepress.com

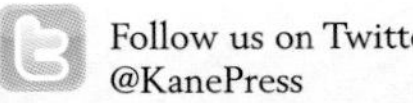
Follow us on Twitter @KanePress

Like us on Facebook facebook.com/kanepress

Y0-BEE-729

A Note for Parents and Teachers

A focus on phonics helps beginning readers gain skill and confidence with reading. Each story in the Bright Owl Books series highlights one vowel sound—for *Princess Pig*, it's the short "i" sound. At the end of the book, you'll find three Story Starters, just for fun. Story Starters are open-ended questions that can be used as a jumping-off place for conversation, storytelling, and imaginative writing.

At Kane Press, we believe the most important part of any reading program is the shared experience of a good story. We hope you'll enjoy *Princess Pig* with a child you love!

Eastern Oklahoma District Library System

KAZUKI TAKAHASHI

MR. ITO, THANK YOU FOR ALL YOUR HARD WORK ON *YU-GI-OH! R*. I'M VERY GRATEFUL THAT YOU'VE CONTINUED IN THE *YU-GI-OH!* TRADITION! I'LL BE LOOKING FORWARD TO YOUR ORIGINAL WORK NEXT! READERS, PLEASE CONTINUE TO SUPPORT MR. ITO IN THE FUTURE!

Artist/author Kazuki Takahashi first tried to break into the manga business in 1982, but success eluded him until *Yu-Gi-Oh!* debuted in the Japanese *Weekly Shonen Jump* magazine in 1996. *Yu-Gi-Oh!*'s themes of friendship and fighting, together with Takahashi's weird and imaginative monsters, soon became enormously successful, spawning a real-world card game, video games and four anime series (two Japanese *Yu-Gi-Oh!* series, *Yu-Gi-Oh! GX* and *Yu-Gi-Oh! 5D's*). A lifelong gamer, Takahashi enjoys shogi (Japanese chess), mahjong, card games and tabletop RPGs, among other games.

AKIRA ITO

THIS IS THE END OF THE "TENMA UPRISING" STORYLINE. THIS SERIES RAN FOR JUST UNDER FOUR YEARS, AND I'M VERY HONORED TO HAVE BEEN A PART OF THE *YU-GI-OH!* WORLD FOR THAT TIME. THANK YOU TO EVERYONE WHO'S SUPPORTED ME.

Akira Ito worked on the original *Yu-Gi-Oh!* manga as an assistant to Kazuki Takahashi. He also assisted in the creation of *Yu-Gi-Oh! GX*. *Yu-Gi-Oh! R* is his first work as lead creator.

Eufaula Memorial Library
301 S. FIRST STREET
EUFAULA, OK 74432

Volume 5
SHONEN JUMP Manga Edition

Original Concept/Supervised by KAZUKI TAKAHASHI
Story and Art by AKIRA ITO

Translation & English Adaptation TAYLOR ENGEL AND IAN REID, HC LANGUAGE SOLUTIONS
Touch-up Art & Lettering ERIC ERBES
Cover Design COURTNEY UTT
Interior Design DANIEL PORTER
Editor JASON THOMPSON

VP, Production ALVIN LU
VP, Sales & Product Marketing GONZALO FERREYRA
VP, Creative LINDA ESPINOSA
Publisher HYOE NARITA

YU-GI-OH! R © 2004 by Kazuki Takahashi, Akira Ito. All rights reserved. First published in Japan in 2004 by SHUEISHA Inc., Tokyo. English translation rights arranged by SHUEISHA Inc.

The stories, characters and incidents mentioned in this publication are entirely fictional.

No portion of this book may be reproduced or transmitted in any form or by any means without written permission from the copyright holders.

Printed in the U.S.A.

Published by VIZ Media, LLC
P.O. Box 77010
San Francisco, CA 94107

10 9 8 7 6 5 4 3 2 1
First printing, June 2010

www.viz.com

PARENTAL ADVISORY
YU-GI-OH! R is rated T for Teen and is recommended for ages 13 and up. Contains fantasy violence.
ratings.viz.com

www.shonenjump.com

VOLUME 5

THE END OF THE BATTLE

Original Concept/Supervised by KAZUKI TAKAHASHI

CAST & STORY

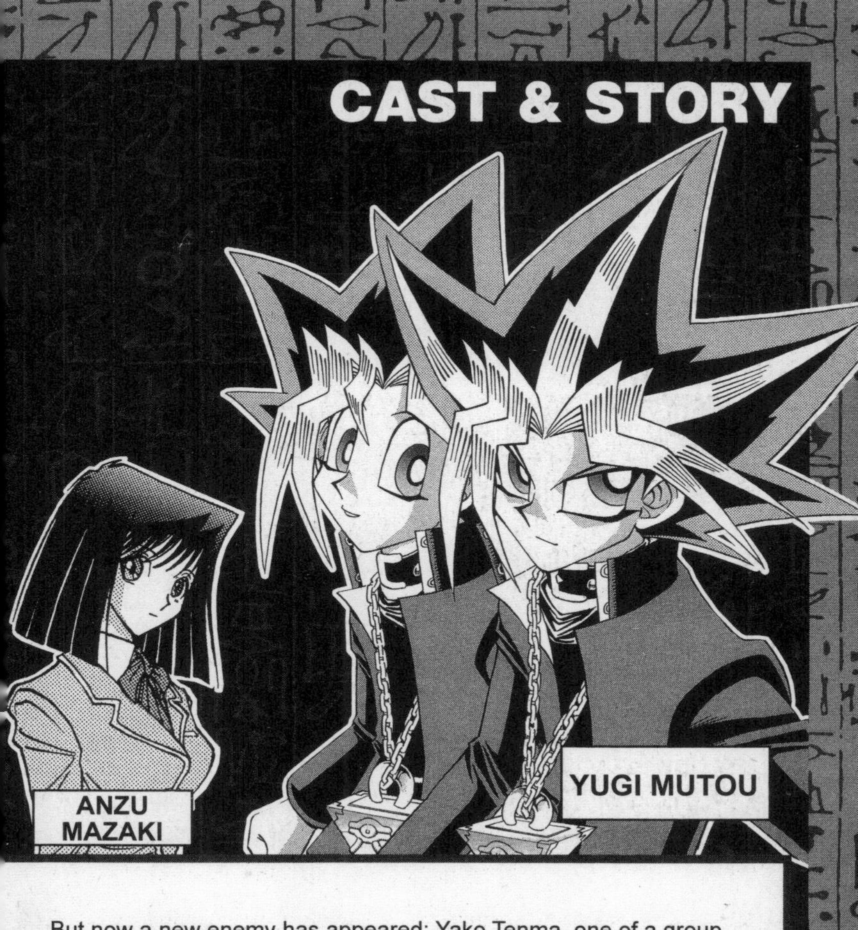

But now a new enemy has appeared: Yako Tenma, one of a group of duelists trained by Pegasus. To avenge his master's death, Yako kidnaps Yugi's friend Anzu, intending to use her for the diabolical "R.A." Project… resurrecting Pegasus's spirit in Anzu's body! With the help of Yako's brother Gekko, Yugi and his friends fight their way through Pegasus's minions, but Yako's three Evil God Cards make him nearly unbeatable. Even Kaiba—Yugi's sometimes rival sometimes ally—falls to Yako. Can anyone stop Yako's madness, or will the Evil Gods reign over all?

When tenth grader Yugi solved the Millennium Puzzle, another spirit took up residence in his body… Yu-Gi-Oh, the King of Games! Using his gaming skills, Yugi fought ruthless adversaries like Maximillion Pegasus, multimillionaire creator of the collectible card game Duel Monsters, and Seto Kaiba, the teenage president of Kaiba Corporation. After winning the Battle City tournament, Yugi acquired the most powerful cards in the world: the three Egyptian God Cards “Slifer the Sky Dragon,” “Obelisk the Tormentor” and “The Winged Dragon of Ra,” which were created by Pegasus based on a mysterious ancient Egyptian card game.

VOLUME 5

THE END OF THE BATTLE

DO YOU SEE THAT BLACK DUEL DISK ON KEITH'S ARM?

THAT BLACK DUEL DISK IS THE ONLY ONE OF ITS KIND. ONLY ONE PERSON IS ALLOWED TO WEAR IT.
THE HIGHEST-RANKING MEMBER OF THE CARD PROFESSOR GUILD!

IF KEITH HAS THAT DISK...
...THEN HE'S BEATEN RICHIE MERCED, THE FORMER CHAMPION.

BE CAREFUL!

WILL DO!

Duel Round 33: Rematch!! Keith vs. Jonouchi

DING

KA-SHUNK

HEY, JONO-UCHI...
HM?

LISTEN!
ANZU'S HEAVY. I CAN'T CARRY HER BY MYSELF.
HONDA... I'M GONNA TELL HER YOU SAID THAT...

JUST HURRY UP AND COME FIND US, OKAY?
YOU GOT IT!

DASH

DON'T YOU DARE LOSE!

Duel Round 33:

Rematch!! Keith vs. Jonouchi

G-
G-
HEYA, KEITH! LONG TIME NO SEE!
G-
G-

SO, YOU'RE TENMA'S FLUNKY NOW? WHATEVER HAPPENED TO THE OLD KEITH FROM DUELIST KINGDOM, WHO WAS THE BOSS OF HIS *OWN* GANG OF STOOGES?

@#$% $#@%!
THAT TENMA &%$#'S GOT NOTHING TO DO WITH THIS!

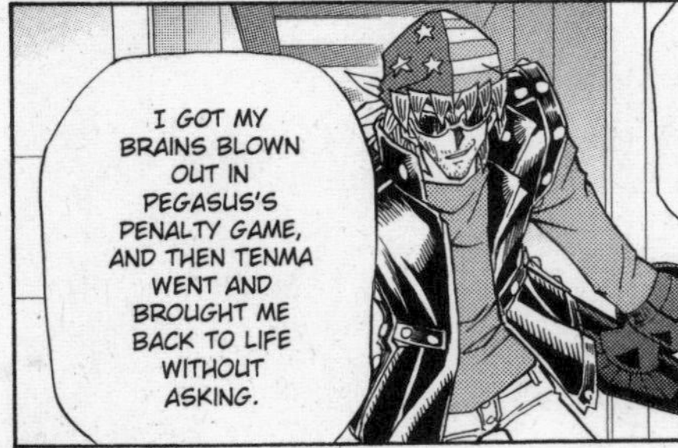
WELL... I GUESS THAT'S BEING UNFAIR...
I GOT MY BRAINS BLOWN OUT IN PEGASUS'S PENALTY GAME, AND THEN TENMA WENT AND BROUGHT ME BACK TO LIFE WITHOUT ASKING.

BUT HEY, I'M ALIVE, SO WHO CARES HOW IT HAPPENED?

!!

IS HE SAYING HE DIED AND CAME BACK...?!
FOR REAL...?

BUT HERE I AM, BACK TO LIFE, AND I FIND OUT THAT @$#%@ PEGASUS IS DEAD ALREADY...

SO TELL ME, WHO AM I SUPPOSED TO GET REVENGE ON, HUH?
!!

HEH HEH HEH... THAT'S THE THING ABOUT GRUDGES.
FOR SOMEONE WHO'S GOT NOTHING LEFT TO LIVE FOR... SOMEONE LIKE ME, WHO WASN'T EVEN ALIVE...
GRUDGES GIVE YOU A REASON TO LIVE!

YEAH...
THAT'S RIGHT ...

YOU AND PEGASUS RUINED ME, JONOUCHI!
I CAME BACK FROM THE DEAD TO GET PAYBACK!

...IS THAT WHEN I WAS OVER ON "THE OTHER SIDE"...
...I MET PEGASUS!

LISTEN! IT WASN'T EASY TO GET A SECOND CHANCE TO DESTROY YOU!
...

THE ONLY REASON I COULD...

NO WAY! ARE YOU SERIOUS ?!
HA! %$@##%$ IDIOT! OF COURSE NOT!
I DON'T REMEMBER ANYTHING FROM WHEN I WAS DEAD!
RRGH... WHY, YOU...

BUT GET THIS... TENMA WAS STARVED FOR INFORMATION ABOUT PEGASUS!
IT WAS THE PERFECT BAIT...!

THAT STUPID KID BELIEVED ANYTHING I TOLD HIM!

WHEN I TOLD HIM THAT PEGASUS WAS KILLED BY YUGI MUTOU...
...YOU AND YOUR BUDDIES WERE SHORT-LISTED AS SACRIFICES FOR THE R.A. PROJECT!

HA HA HA! PRETTY $#%&% SMART, HUH?
I KNEW THAT IF I FOUND YUGI, I'D FIND YOU RIGHT ON HIS TAIL, JUST LIKE ALWAYS!

WA HA HA HA HA HA!

BAM
YOU SEE? SEE ALL THE TROUBLE I WENT THROUGH?
YOU BETTER FIGHT LIKE YOU MEAN IT!!

SO...

WHAT YOU'RE SAYING IS, YOU WANTED TO DUEL ME...
...SO YOU MADE TENMA TARGET YUGI AND ANZU.

HEH HEH...

FOR *THAT* YOU NEARLY KILLED ANZU...?
CLENCH

YEAH, I'LL FIGHT YOU!!
I'LL KICK YOU RIGHT BACK DOWN TO HELL!

MAN, HAVE I BEEN WAITING FOR THIS...!

COME ON! LET'S DUEL!
MY TURN!
I DRAW!
KEITH HOWARD
Life Points 4000
I SET ONE CARD FACE-DOWN!
BAM
KATSUYA JONOUCHI
Life Points 4000

THEN I SUMMON LITTLE-WINGUARD IN DEFENSE MODE!
BAM
LITTLE-WINGUARD
ATK 1400 DEF 1800
TURN OVER!
BRING IT ON, CREEP!
HAW HAW HAW...
MY TURN...
I PLAY ONE CARD FACE DOWN...
RAM
MOTOR SHELL!! DEFENSE MODE!!
DOOM
MOTOR SHELL
When this card is destroyed and sent from the field to the Graveyard, Special Summon 1 "Motor Parts Token" (Machine-Type/DARK/Level 1/ATK 0/DEF 0).
ATK 1300 DEF 1800

THAT ENDS MY TURN...

WHAT?! IS THAT ALL?!
FOR SOME-ONE WHO WAS TALKING SO BIG, THAT MONSTER LOOKS PRETTY WIMPY!

HEH HEH HEH...
I'VE BEEN WAITING A LONG TIME TO FINISH YOU OFF.

RMMMBB
IT'D BE BORING IF I ENDED THINGS TOO QUICKLY!

THAT JERK... HE WAS CREEPY BEFORE...
...BUT HE'S WAY WEIRDER NOW...

BUT WHO CARES?! THIS JERK MESSED WITH MY FRIENDS!
NO WAY AM I LETTING HIM GET TO ME!!
MY TURN!!

BOOM
I SUMMON PANTHER WARRIOR!
PANTHER WARRIOR
ATK 2000 DEF 1600
GO GET HIM!
ATTACK MOTOR SHELL!!
ROAR
HE HASN'T CHANGED. ALL HIS ATTACKS ARE SIMPLE AND SHORT-SIGHTED...
@#$%!! I CAN'T BELIEVE I EVER LOST TO A GUY LIKE THIS!
IT DRIVES ME CRAZY!
FACE-DOWN CARD, REVEAL!

BAM
EQUIP SPELL CARD "ENGINE TUNER"!!
MOTOR SHELL GETS A TUNE-UP!
SKRIK SKRIK
KLAK KLAK
SKWEEK SKWEEK
ENGINE TUNER (EQUIP SPELL CARD)
A monster equipped with this card cannot be switched to Defense Position. The equipped monster has its ATK increased by an amount equal to half of its DEF. When the monster equipped with this card is destroyed, this card remains on the field and can be activated again during your Main Phase.
MOTOR SHELL ATK 2200
ITS ATTACK POWER GOES UP, AND IT GOES OUT OF DEFENSE MODE!
KLANNGG
MOTOR SHELL COUNTER-ATTACKS!!
KA
BAM
MM
PANTHER WARRIOR IS DESTROYED!!
ZSSH
OUCH...
KATSUYA JONOUCHI Life Points 4000 ↓ 3800

WA HA HA HA HA HA!
WHAT'S WRONG, JOEY? YOU REALLY ARE AN AMATEUR, AIN'TCHA?
HEY, SHOVE IT! THIS "AMATEUR" KICKED YOUR BUTT LAST TIME, REMEMBER?!
BESIDES, I'M NOT AN AMATEUR!
DANG IT...!
I'LL SET ONE CARD FACE DOWN...
...AND END MY TURN!
BANG
HUH ...
BACK TO ME THEN!
I'LL PLAY A FACE-DOWN CARD TOO...
BAM
...THEN ATTACK YOUR DEFENSIVE MONSTER!
WA
CANNON BALL!!
THOOM

I ACTIVATE MY FACE-DOWN SPELL CARD!!
HAH!
TA DA
FAIRY BOX!
FAIRY BOX
(SPELL CARD)
Each time a monster on your opponent's side of the field attacks, toss a coin and call Heads or Tails. If you call right, the attacking monster's ATK becomes 0 only during the Battle Phase.
YIKES ...!
WHAT ?!
YOUR MONSTER HID IN THE BOX?! WHAT KIND OF $#@% CARD IS THAT?!
THAT'S CALLED STRATEGY! SEE, YOUR MONSTER DIDN'T EVEN SCRATCH HIM!
WA HA HA HA HA HA HA!
@#$% ...
THINKS HE'S SO SMART...
GET READY! IT'S MY TURN!

SO I GOTTA BEAT YOUR FOUR-STAR MONSTER...
I KNOW JUST WHAT I NEED!
I SACRIFICE LITTLE-WINGUARD AND SUMMON...
DIVINE KNIGHT ISHZARK !!
DIVINE KNIGHT ISHZARK
ATK 2300 DEF 1800
CUT MOTOR SHELL IN TWO!
GRR...
KEITH HOWARD
Life Points 4000
↓
3900

ALL RIGHT! HOW DOES THAT FEEL?

IT FEELS GOOD ...
DID YOU FORGET THAT MOTOR SHELL LEAVES A PART ON THE FIELD WHEN IT'S DESTROYED?

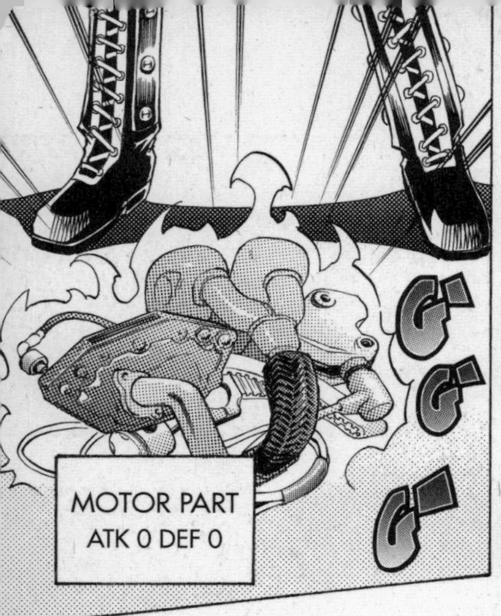
MOTOR PART
ATK 0 DEF 0

ZM
ZM
ZM
ON TOP OF THAT, THIS EQUIP CARD STAYS ON THE FIELD TOO.
ENGINE TUNER
(EQUIP MAGIC CARD)
A monster equipped with this card cannot be switched to defense position. The equipped monster has its ATK increased by an amount equal to half of its DEF. When the monster equipped with this card is destroyed, this card remains on the field and can be activated again during your main phase.

HEH HEH HEH...
IT'S JUST WAITING FOR A NEW MONSTER TO EQUIP!

...

OKAY! I SET ONE CARD FACE DOWN!
TURN OVER!

MY TURN!
@#$%... MOTOR SHELL LEFT ME SOME GOOD STUFF!
CHECK THIS OUT!
GWRRRR
I SACRIFICE MOTOR PART...
...AND SUMMON MOTOR VIOLENCE!!
MOTOR VIOLENCE
★★★★★★
When this card is destroyed and sent from the field to the Graveyard, Special Summon 2 "Motor Parts Tokens" (Machine-Type/DARK/Level 1/ATK 0/ DEF 0).
ATK 2100 DEF 1200

THE ENGINE TUNERS GO TO WORK ON MOTOR VIOLENCE! NOW IT'S EVEN STRONGER!
ENGINE TUNER
(EQUIP SPELL CARD)
A monster equipped with this card cannot be switched to Defense Position. The equipped monster has its ATK increased by an amount equal to half of its DEF. When the monster equipped with this card is destroyed, this card remains on the field and can be activated again during your Main Phase.
2700 ATTACK POINTS!!
THAT'S AS POWERFUL AS A SEVEN-STAR MONSTER!
THOOM
THOOM
MOTOR VIOLENCE ATK 2700
MOTOR VIOLENCE, ATTACK!!
MOTOR CANNON!!!
MMM

WA HA HA HA HA!
BLEW 'EM CLEAN AWAY!
FWOOOO
WH... WHAT THE--?!
WHAT'S THAT THING?!
NO WAY! TIME MACHINE ...!
HEY! THAT'S MY CARD! I'VE BEEN LOOKING FOR IT!
YOU ROTTEN...

HUH?
YOU MEAN THIS CARD I JUST ACTIVATED?
AFTER I BEAT YOU AT DUELIST KINGDOM...
...YOU GOT MAD, THREW YOUR DECK DOWN AND RAN OFF! REMEMBER?
I FIGURED YOU DIDN'T CARE, SO I HELPED MYSELF TO THIS CARD!
YOU... YOU LITTLE BRAT...
TIME MACHINE
(TRAP CARD)
Activate only when a monster is destroyed by battle and sent to the Graveyard. Special Summon that monster to the same side of the field it was on, in the same battle position it was in when destroyed.
BIG DEAL!
ALL YOU DID IS BRING BACK THE SAME ISHZARK FROM A TURN AGO! IT DOESN'T CHANGE HIS ATTACK POWER!
I'LL JUST TAKE HIM OUT AGAIN!!
MAN, DON'T YOU EVEN KNOW HOW TO USE THAT THING?!
WHAT A @#$%$ AMATEUR!
OH YEAH?
KLANK
D-
D-
D-

DOOM
CHECK THIS OUT, STUPID!
I ACTIVATED ANOTHER SPELL CARD!
WHAT ...?!
I SPECIAL SUMMONED ISHZARK, SO NOW I CAN SWAP HIM OUT WITH ANOTHER SPECIAL SUMMONED MONSTER!
BAM
TAKE OVER!
TAKE OVER
(SPELL CARD)
Activate only when you perform a successful Special Summon. Tribute the Summoned monster and Special Summon 1 monster from your hand of the same Type.

AND THE MONSTER I SUMMON IS...
BAM
GILFORD THE LIGHTNING !!
GILFORD THE LIGHTNING
You can Tribute 3 monsters to Tribute Summon this card. If you do, destroy all monsters your opponent controls.
ATK 2800 DEF 1400
GILFORD THE LIGHTNING!!
SO! AFTER I WIN THIS DUEL...
...WHAT SHOULD I TAKE FROM YOU NEXT?!
MOTOR VIOLENCE IS DESTROYED!
!!

DUEL ROUND 34: THE LAST JASHIN RISES!!
I USED TIME MACHINE TO SUMMON GILFORD THE LIGHTNING!
MOTOR VIOLENCE IS NO MATCH FOR IT!
TIME MACHINE
(TRAP CARD)
Activate only when a monster is destroyed by battle and sent to the Graveyard. Special Summon that monster to the same side of the field it was on, in the same battle position it was in when destroyed.
GILFORD THE
KEITH HOWARD
Life Points 3800
RRGH ...!

ALL RIGHT, KEITH!
I HOPE YOU'RE PREPARED TO ANTE UP AN EVEN BETTER CARD AFTER THIS GAME!
YOU LITTLE @#&%... *YOU'RE* GOING TO TAKE MORE OF *MY* CARDS...?

HEH HEH HEH!
HEY, KEITH! I LIKE YOUR ACCES-SORIES!
WHAT ?!

THAT THING ON YOUR ARM!
THAT BLACK DUEL DISK!
!!

YOU KNOW WHO THAT DISK WOULD LOOK BETTER ON?
ME, OBVI-OUSLY. RIGHT?!

YEAH... LAUGH WHILE YOU CAN, YOU LITTLE...

Duel Round 34: The Last Jashin Rises!!

...
BACK AT DUELIST KINGDOM, I DIDN'T REALLY HAVE TACTICS. I GUESS I WAS AN AMATEUR THEN.

BUT...
WHILE YOU WERE WASTING TIME BEING DEAD...
...I MET ALL SORTS OF DUELISTS... AND I'VE GROWN!

YOU'RE SEEING THE NEW AND IMPROVED JONOUCHI!

AND YOU LOST TO ME WHEN I WAS AN AMATEUR, SO THERE'S NO WAY YOU CAN BEAT ME NOW!
WA HA HA HA HA!

RRGH ...

...
THAAAAT'S RIGHT, JONOUCHI... GO AHEAD, BE OVER-CONFIDENT...

MOTOR VIOLENCE
★★★★★★
When this card is destroyed and sent from the field to the Graveyard, Special Summon 2 "Motor Parts Tokens" (Machine-Type/DARK/Level 1/ATK 0/DEF 0).
ATK 2100 DEF 1200
WHEN MOTOR VIOLENCE WAS DESTROYED, IT LEFT TWO PARTS ON THE FIELD...

THE ONLY PROBLEM IS, SINCE THE PARTS AREN'T REALLY CARDS...
...I CAN'T PUT 'EM IN DEFENSE MODE...

D- D-
DO OM

WELL, IT DOESN'T MATTER...
SNEER

DA DO OM
AND THE CARD UP MY SLEEVE IS...

SLIP...

I'VE USED THIS TRICK BEFORE, BUT...
...I'VE GOT A CARD SQUIRRELED AWAY IN MY WRISTBAND!

A TRAP CARD, RING OF DESTRUCTION!

RING OF DESTRUCTION
(TRAP CARD)
Destroy 1 face-up monster and inflict damage to the owner equal to its ATK.

THIS CARD IS BRUTAL. IT DESTROYS A MONSTER AND DAMAGES THE PLAYER!

BEFORE I END MY TURN...

OPEN WIDE, JONOUCHI!

BAM

I'LL PLAY ONE CARD FROM MY HAND FACE DOWN!

BEEEEEEP

WHAT THE--?!

BEEEEP

BEEEEP

WH... WHAT ...?!

NO WAY... CHEAT PREVEN-TION...
IT WON'T TAKE ANY CARDS EXCEPT ONES I DRAW FROM MY DECK?!
B-BMP
HEY HEY HEY!
YOU JERK! YOU JUST TRIED TO CHEAT, DIDN'T YOU!
FWIP
I GUESS YOU'RE GETTIN' PRETTY NERVOUS SEEING HOW FAR I'VE COME SINCE DUELIST KINGDOM!
MY TURN!
D-D-D
GILFORD, ATTACK!
FWOOOOOOOM
GILFORD DESTROYS ONE OF THE MOTOR PARTS!

MOTOR PARTS HAVE AN ATTACK OF ZERO! THAT MEANS YOU TAKE ALL THE DAMAGE!
@#$&
...!
FOOM
KEITH HOWARD
Life Points 3800
↓
1000

THAT'S WHAT YOU GET FOR TRYING SOME-THING THAT LAME!
WA HA HA HA HA!

THAT LOUSY LITTLE RICH KID! WHY'D HE HAVE TO GO AND DO THAT?
THAT'S GONNA MAKE THINGS HARD...!

I SET TWO MORE CARDS ON THE FIELD!

HEH HEH HEH... THE CARDS I JUST SET FACE DOWN ARE TIME WIZARD AND PROBABILITY CHANGE!
TIME WIZARD
(SPELL CARD)

PROBABILITY CHANGE
(TRAP CARD)
Redo the results of any random effect (coin toss, dice roll, roulette or slot machine).

AFTER TIME MACHINE COMES TIME MAGIC!
TURN OVER!!

WITH THESE TWO CARDS, I'LL TURN YOUR NEXT MONSTER TO SCRAP, NO MATTER WHAT IT IS!

THIS MATCH IS IN THE BAG!!
HEH HEH HEH...

HEY, KEITH! IF YOU'VE GOTTA CHEAT ALREADY...
...DOES THAT MEAN YOU'VE GOT NO CHANCE?
C'MON, SURRENDER !!

...

...
DID YOU SAY... SURRENDER...?

SURRENDER...? ME...?

HEH...
HEH... HEH HEH HEH...

YOUR WIN AT DUELIST KINGDOM WAS A COMPLETE FLUKE...
...BUT IT LOOKS LIKE IT GAVE YOU A REAL #$%@%$ EGO.

YOU'RE TELLING ME TO GIVE UP?!
BAM
ME, THE GREAT BANDIT KEITH, THE NUMBER ONE CARD PROFESSOR !!

SHUT YOUR MOUTH BEFORE I SHUT IT FOR YOU!!
FWIP
I SACRIFICE MOTOR PART...
...AND SUMMON MOTOR KAISER!!
DOOOM
I ALSO PLAY ONE CARD FACE DOWN!
BAM
TURN END!
MOTOR KAISER
ATK 2000 DEF 1400
MOTOR KAISER
ATK 2700
(Equip card "Engine Tuner" in effect)

HA!
GETTING ALL DRAMATIC OVER A LITTLE MONSTER LIKE THAT?!
GILFORD THE LIGHTNING WILL EAT THAT THING FOR BREAKFAST!!
HERE GOES!
IT'S MY TURN! I ATTACK!
I'LL FINISH YOU OFF ON THIS TURN, KEITH!
BUT FIRST, I'LL ACTIVATE MY FACE-DOWN CARD...
TAKE THAT!! TIME MAGIC!

KA
SHIIING
KA
SHIIING
BA
WH... WHAT'S THAT?!
MY CARDS ARE CHAINED DOWN?!
BAM
THAT'S RIGHT!
I USED MY FACE-DOWN CARD!
CARD HEXATIVE!!
BA
M
CARD HEXATIVE
(SPELL CARD)
Select any number of face-down Spell or Trap Cards on the field. The selected Spell or Trap Cards cannot be activated as long as they remain on the field.
IT KEEPS YOUR CARDS PINNED TO THE FIELD!
RGGH...
WELL, YOU STILL CAN'T STOP GILFORD THE LIGHTNING!

ZASH
LIGHTNING CRASH SWORD!!
MOTOR KAISER GOES DOWN!
KEITH HOWARD
Life Points 1000
900

READ THIS WAY

THAT MOVE WAS POINTLESS! I DON'T KNOW WHY YOU EVEN BOTHERED!
FSSH
HH
BUT I SHAVED SOME MORE LIFE POINTS OFF YA!

...
YEAH? SO WHAT?

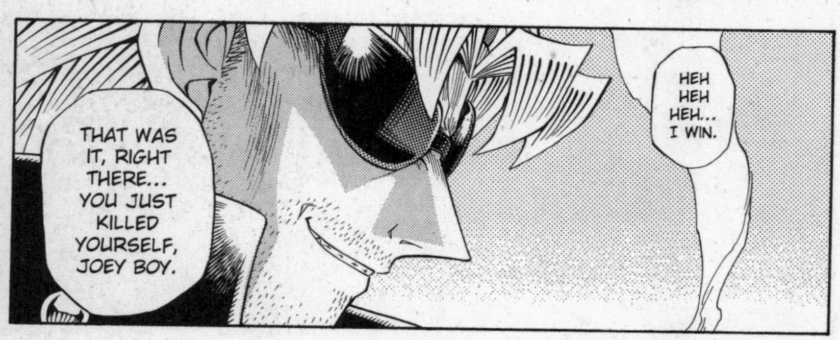

HEH HEH HEH... I WIN.
THAT WAS IT, RIGHT THERE... YOU JUST KILLED YOURSELF, JOEY BOY.

HUH?!
WHAT'RE YOU TALKING ABOUT? YOUR FIELD'S COMPLETELY EMPTY! LOOK BEFORE YOU SAY STUFF!

YOU DUMB #$#@%...
USE YOUR EYES AND TAKE A GOOD LOOK AT... THIS!
VOOM

DA-DOOM

FACE-DOWN TRAP CARD, "SCRAP GARAGE" !!

THIS CARD LETS ME RETURN ALL THE MOTOR MONSTERS IN MY GRAVEYARD TO THE FIELD!

SCRAP GARAGE

(TRAP CARD)

Activate only when a "Motor" monster on your side of the field is destroyed and sent to the Graveyard. Special Summon as many of your "Motor" monsters as possible from your Graveyard to your side of the field in Attack Position. The ATK and DEF of all monsters Summoned by this card's effect become 0.

THEIR ATTACK AND DEFENSE POINTS ARE ZERO, AND THEY'VE GOT NO SPECIAL ABILITIES, BUT STILL!
MOTOR KAISER, MOTOR PARTS
ATK 0 DEF 0

HE JUST GOT THREE MONSTERS ONTO THE FIELD IN AN INSTANT...

ZM ZM ZM ZM
THERE'S THREE OF THEM! AND THAT'S WHAT COUNTS!
DO YOU GET IT? KNOW WHAT THIS MEANS ...?

HEH HEH HEH...
...
I'M GONNA SHOW YOU SOME-THING GOOD...
A REAL GOD... AN EVIL GOD...
GWRRRRRR
MY TURN!
I SACRIFICE ALL THE SCRAP MONSTERS AND SUMMON...
HO OM

THE WICKED ERASER !!!
THE WICKED ERASER
★★★★★★★★★★
This card cannot be Special Summoned. This card cannot be Normal Summoned or Set except by Tributing 3 monsters. The ATK and DEF of this card are each equal to the number of cards your opponent controls x 1000. When this card is destroyed and sent to the Graveyard, destroy all cards on the field. During your Main Phase, you can destroy this card.
ATK ? DEF ?

A J... JASHIN! AN EVIL GOD!
MEET THE WICKED ERASER!
WA HA HA HA HA HA!
IT'S THE SAME KIND OF MONSTER AS THE GOD CARDS YOUR PAL YUGI HAS!

SO TENMA'S WICKED AVATAR WASN'T THE ONLY EVIL GOD? THERE WAS THIS THING TOO...!
THE WICKED ERASER'S ATTACK POINTS ARE 1000 TIMES THE NUMBER OF CARDS ON YOUR FIELD!
WHAT ...?!
THAT MEANS RIGHT NOW ITS ATTACK POWER IS 3000!
EAT THIS, JONOUCHI !!
THAT JERK! SO THAT'S WHY HE CHAINED DOWN MY FACE-DOWN CARDS...!

DOOOOOO
DIGESTIVE BREATH!!!
NGGH ...!
P

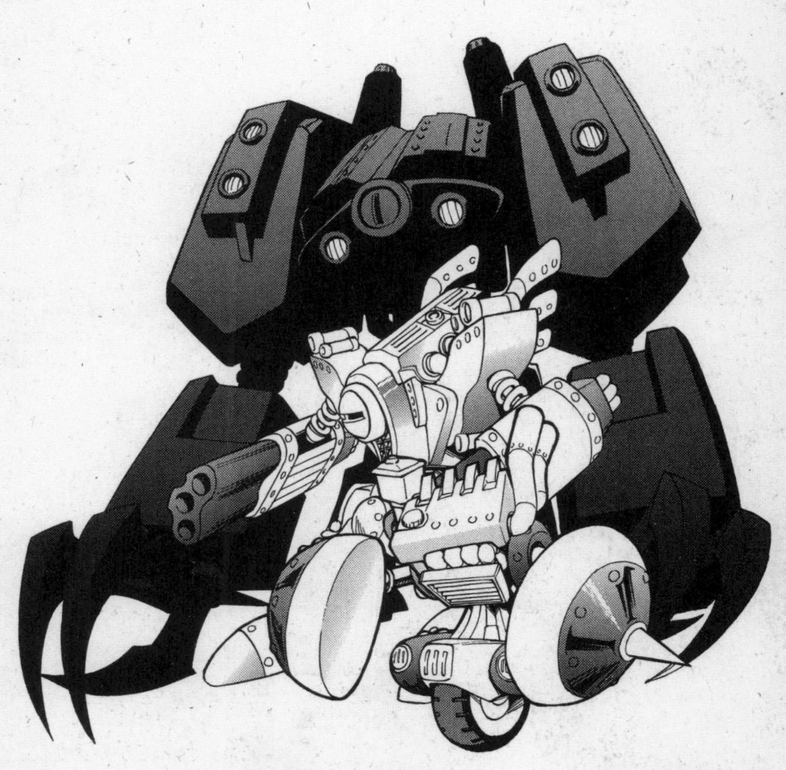

Duel Round 35: Jonouchi Strikes Back!!

SO THIS IS... AN EVIL GOD ...!
OM
WA HA HA HA HA HA HA HA!
THE WICKED ERASER
This card cannot be Special Summoned. This card cannot be Normal Summoned or Set except by Tributing 3 monsters. The ATK and DEF of this card are each equal to the number of cards your opponent controls x 1000. When this card is destroyed and sent to the Graveyard, destroy all cards on the field. During your Main Phase, you can destroy this card.
ATK ? DEF ?
DUEL ROUND 35:
JONOUCHI STRIKES BACK!!

THE WICKED... ERASER...
IT'S LIKE TENMA'S "AVATAR" THING...
A MONSTER JUST AS STRONG AS YUGI'S EGYPTIAN GODS...

THE WICKED ERASER'S ATTACK POINTS ARE EQUAL TO THE NUMBER OF CARDS ON YOUR FIELD!
GILFORD THE LIGHTNING IS NOTHING BUT MELTED MEAT...
...BUT YOU'VE STILL GOT THE TWO FACE-DOWN CARDS I CHAINED TO YOUR FIELD!
!!
THAT PUTS THE ERASER'S ATTACK POINTS AT 2000!
FWOOOOO
WHATSAMATTER, SCARED? I THOUGHT A GOD CARD WAS NO PROBLEM FOR THE BIG BAD JONOUCHI!
GRR...

READ THIS WAY

HIS ATTACK IS 2000 NOW... BUT IF I SUMMON A MONSTER TO FIGHT HIM...
...HIS ATTACK WILL GO UP TO 3000...

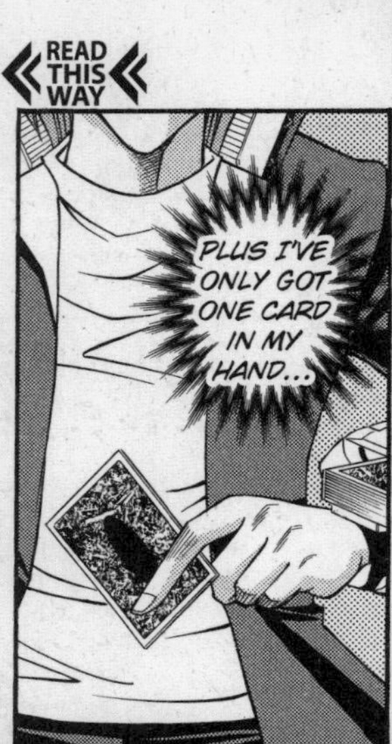

PLUS I'VE ONLY GOT ONE CARD IN MY HAND...

DANGIT...! WHAT DO I DO...?
MY TURN! DRAW!
FWP

HEH HEH HEH...
BAM
M
TAKE THIS!
...
SORRY, KEITH!!
LOOKS LIKE I ALREADY DREW A CARD THAT CAN FINISH OFF YOUR GOD!
GIANT TRUNADE
(SPELL CARD)
Return all Spell and Trap Cards on the field to their owners' hands.
GWOO
OO
SPELL CARD! GIANT TRUNADE!
OO
OO
THIS CARD TAKES ALL SPELL AND TRAP CARDS OFF THE FIELD!

THAT GIVES ME MY CARDS BACK...
...AND BECAUSE THERE'S NO MORE CARDS ON THE FIELD, YOUR EVIL GOD'S ATTACK POINTS DROP TO ZERO!
OH YEAH! WHO'S THE MAN?!
HWO
OO
WA HA HA HA HA HA!
@#$%...
FACE-DOWN SPELL CARD, ACTIVATE!
BA
DE-SPELL!
HA...
MI
DE-SPELL
(SPELL CARD)
Cancel the effect of any 1 Spell Card.
THIS CANCELS OUT YOUR GIANT TRUNADE!
BA
M

AW, NO!!
GIANT TRUNADE... MY TRUMP CARD...!
FWOOOO
SH

YOUR TWO FACE-DOWN CARDS ARE STILL ON YOUR FIELD!
THAT MEANS ERASER'S ATTACK POWER IS STILL 2000!

DANG IT!
HEH...

THE WICKED ERASER...

THE STUPID THING'S SUPPOSED TO BE MY SERVANT, BUT ITS ABILITIES GO UP AND DOWN BASED ON MY OPPONENT...
WHAT A LOUSY MONSTER... @#$%...

PLUS, OTHER THAN THIS CARD, I'M USING A MACHINE DECK! MY SPELL CARDS LIKE ENGINE TUNER DON'T AFFECT IT AT ALL!

THAT IDIOT TENMA...

KEITH HOWARD...
YOU WERE BROUGHT BACK INTO THIS WORLD THROUGH THE POWER OF THE EVIL GODS.

THIS, THEN, IS FOR YOU.
KEEP IT WITH YOU ALWAYS AS A REMINDER THAT YOU OWE YOUR LIFE TO THE THREE EVIL GODS...

THAT BRAT... I HATE HAVING TO USE ONE OF TENMA'S MONSTERS!

HEH HEH HEH...

GWAAAA
MY TURN! THE EVIL GOD ATTACKS !!
DIRECT ATTACK ON JONOUCHI!

READ THIS WAY
SHSSH
ARRGH ...!
SHHH
NGH...
KATSUYA JONOUCHI
Life Points 1600
WA HA HA HA HA HA!
OOOOOO
THIS DUEL IS MINE, JOEY BOY!
SQUIRM ALL YOU WANT, BUT YOU CAN'T WIN!
HE'S WAY STRONG...
AND HIS STRENGTH ...
IT'S NOT JUST BECAUSE OF THE GOD CARD...

DOOOOOOOOM

CRUD...! WHAT'S THAT CREEPY FEELING?
PURE HATE...? OR A GRUDGE, LIKE GHOSTS CARRY...?
I'VE GOT NO CLUE... BUT IT AIN'T NORMAL...

STILL...!

IF HE'S GOT A GRUDGE AGAINST ME, HE SHOULD'VE COME TO MY PLACE AND HAD IT OUT WITH ME ONE-ON-ONE!

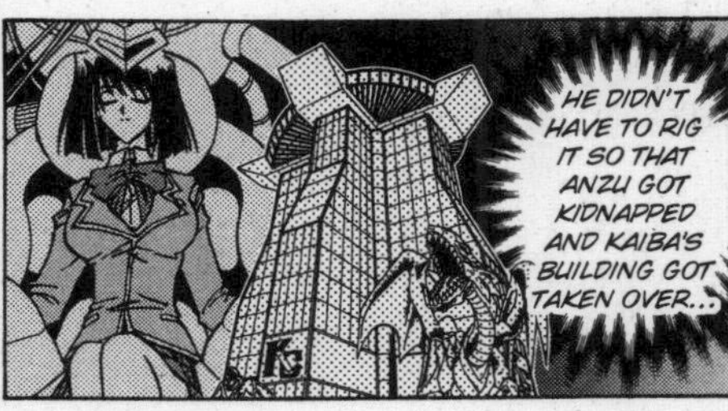
HE DIDN'T HAVE TO RIG IT SO THAT ANZU GOT KIDNAPPED AND KAIBA'S BUILDING GOT TAKEN OVER...

GRIP
THAT SCUMBAG...

AS IF I'M GONNA LOSE TO A JERK LIKE HIM!!

MY TURN!!

I PLAY ONE CARD FACE DOWN!

TURN OVER!

HAW!
ANOTHER FACE-DOWN CARD?! THAT MAKES THREE!

THANKS, JOEY! THAT BOOSTS THE GOD'S ATTACK POWER TO 3000!
THE WICKED ERASER
ATK 3000

I DUNNO WHAT YOU'RE TRYING TO PULL, BUT SPELLS AND TRAPS DON'T WORK ON GOD CARDS!
SO YOU PLAYED A CARD? SO @#$%$ WHAT?!
LIKE THAT'S GONNA SCARE ME?!
SEE HOW MUCH YOUR CARD HELPS WHEN YOUR FACE IS DRIPPING OFF THE BONE!
KILL HIM, ERASER!
POWARP
DIGESTIVE BREATH!!!
RRR
WHAT?!
VWIP

TRAP SPELL CARD! GRAVE-ROBBER!
I'M HELPING MYSELF TO MOTOR VIOLENCE FROM YOUR GRAVEYARD!!
MOTOR VIOLENCE
GRAVEROBBER
(TRAP SPELL CARD)
Select 1 Spell Card from your opponent's Graveyard and add it to your hand.
THE WICKED ERASER'S ATTACK HITS MOTOR VIOLENCE DEAD ON!!
@#$# ...!
AGAIN... YOU TOOK MY CARD AGAIN ...!
YOU SNOT-NOSED LITTLE ...!!
HEH HEH ...

HUH?
I THOUGHT I'D TAKE MORE DAMAGE FROM THAT...
KATSUYA JONOUCHI
Life Points 1600
1300

OH, I GET IT!
MOTOR VIOLENCE PICKED UP THE EFFECT FROM ***YOUR*** ENGINE TUNER CARD, DIDN'T IT?

MAN, DID I LUCK OUT!
MOTOR VIOLENCE
ATK 2700

ENGINE TUNER
(EQUIP SPELL CARD)
A machine monster equipped with this card cannot be switched to Defense Position. The equipped monster has its ATK increased by an amount equal to half of its DEF. When the monster equipped with this card is destroyed, this card remains on the field and is automatically equipped to any machine monster on the field with an ATK higher than 0.

AND THAT'S NOT ALL...

TA
DA

IT LEFT TWO ***MOTOR PARTS*** ON MY FIELD!

KEH... SO I GAVE YOU THE SACRIFICES TO SUMMON A HIGH-LEVEL MONSTER, HUH...?
BUT SO WHAT?! YOU GOT NO GOD CARDS! ARE YOU TELLING ME THERE'S A MONSTER IN YOUR HAND THAT'S STRONGER THAN GILFORD THE LIGHTNING?!
NOPE.
FORGET MY HAND, I DON'T HAVE A MONSTER STRONGER THAN GILFORD THE LIGHTNING IN MY ENTIRE DECK...
LIKE I SAID... I DON'T HAVE A STRONGER CARD...
...BUT MAYBE YOU DO!
BAM
PFAH!
GWA HA HA HA HAA!
MY TURN...

A MONSTER FROM MY HAND...?! THAT @#$%@ CARD... IT'S TOTALLY OVERPOWERED...!

BADUMP

WH... WHAT?!

SPELL CARD! SUMMON CAPTURE!

SUMMON CAPTURE (SPELL CARD)

Look at your opponent's hand and select 1 Monster Card from it.

HEH HEH HEH... YOU GOT A LOT OF NICE CARDS, DON'TCHA?
GRR...

!!
C'MON, C'MON, SHOW ME YOUR HAND!

OKAY...

YOU LITTLE PIECE OF...!
HEY! WATCH IT!
SWING

FWIP
ALL RIGHT!
I'LL TAKE THIS ONE!

I SACRIFICE THE TWO MOTOR PARTS...
...AND SUMMON THIS GUY!
SWRRRRR
FIENDISH ENGINE Ω
ATK 2800 DEF 2000
FIENDISH ENGINE OMEGA !!!

AND THAT'S NOT ALL! THANKS TO THE EFFECT OF YOUR ENGINE TUNER CARD, IT'S GOT AN ATTACK POWER OF 3800!
ENGINE TUNER
(EQUIP SPELL CARD)
A machine monster equipped with this card cannot be switched to Defense Position. The equipped monster has its ATK increased by an amount equal to half of its DEF. When the monster equipped with this card is destroyed, this card remains on the field and is automatically equipped to any machine monster on the field with an ATK higher than 0.
FIENDISH ENGINE Ω
ATK 3800
ZWMM
THAT'S MORE ATTACK POWER THAN YOUR GOD!
THE WICKED ERASER
ATK 3000
WA HA HA HA HA HA!
HMPH! WHATEVER...
I WAS JUST THINKING HOW BORING IT WOULD BE IF I WON WITH THE ERASER!

KEEP LIP-FLAPPIN' ALL YOU WANT!

I'LL BE BUSY KICKING YOUR BUTT!

JONOUCHI CRUSHER !!

(NAME COINED BY JONOUCHI)

D- D- D- D-

FIENDISH ENGINE OMEGA ATTACKS!!
JONOUCHI CRUSHER !!
D
D
D
D
D
D
IS THIS EVEN GONNA WORK...?
DUEL ROUND 36: DEATH OF A GOD!!

BOOOM
MMMM
Duel Round 36: Death of a God!!

DA
IT GOT THROUGH ...!
THUD D D D

ALL RIGHT! I TOOK OUT THE EVIL GOD!!

...
KEITH HOWARD
Life Points 100
NOW YOU'VE DONE IT...

WHAT'S THIS STUFF?!
THE ERASER'S... BLACK... BLOOD?!
SHAAAAA
GLORP
GLORP
BLUB GLUB

KEITH! WHAT'S HAPPENING ?!
HEE... HEE HEE...

BWEH HEH HEH...
HEH HEH... I FORGOT... TO TELL YOU SOME-THING...
SEE, WHEN THE ERASER GOES TO THE GRAVEYARD... IT DRAGS ALL THE OTHER CARDS ON THE FIELD WITH IT...!

HEH HEH... HEE HEE HEE...
GLUB GLUB
B B B

RRGH ...
BUT WHY...?!

THIS IS BAD! I CAN'T LET HIS TURN START WHILE I'M DEFENSE-LESS...

I CAN'T BELIEVE THE ERASER CAN DO THIS...
I GET IT... THAT'S WHY HE DIDN'T PUT ANY CARDS ON HIS FIELD EXCEPT FOR THE ERASER...!

BEFORE I END MY TURN, I SET ONE CARD FACE DOWN...!
BAM
?!
WH...?!
SPLOOSHHH
WAAAAGGH!
THE EVIL GOD'S BLOOD IS COILING AROUND ME...
SPSSHHH
AHH... AGH...

WHAT'S GOING ON...? MY VISION'S GONE COMPLETELY BLACK...

I CAN'T HEAR ANYTHING... CAN'T SMELL ANYTHING...

MY...MY BODY'S LOSING ALL SENSATION...

WH...WHAT IS THIS? WHAT'S HAPPENING TO ME...?

THIS AGAIN...
THIS... THIS FEELING...
HEH HEH... HEH HEE...
HEE ...

J... JOEY...
HEE HEE ...
Y-YOU'RE FEELING WHAT I'M FEELING, RIGHT? THE FEELING OF *DEATH*...

I...

NOW... I'LL FINISH HIM OFF NOW...!
NOW IT'S...MY TURN...

ZM
I ACTI... ACTIVATE ...
THE SPELL CARD... *TWO-FOR-ONE REPAIR JOB!*
ZM
ZM
TWO-FOR-ONE REPAIR JOB
(SPELL CARD)
Special Summon 1 "Motor" monster from your Graveyard to your side of the field. After that, any remaining "Motor" monsters in your Graveyard are removed from play.

HEH HEH HEE... I'LL SUMMON...
...A MONSTER FROM THE DEAD... I'LL SUMMON...

FIENDISH ENGINE Ω!!
JUST DIE, JONOUCHI ...!!!
AHH...
AAGGGH!
OUT OF THE DARK ...!!
SKULL DICE!
FACE-DOWN CARD, REVEAL!
SKULL DICE
(TRAP CARD)
Roll 1 six-sided die. Divide one monster's ATK and DEF by the result.
...
F...

TOSS
FIENDISH ENGINE Ω
ATK 700 (1/4)
NRRGH...!

HWOOOOOO

RRGH ...!

THAT WAS TOO CLOSE... HE ALMOST GOT ME...!

KATSUYA JONOUCHI
Life Points 600

BUT...
...THAT ATTACK WOKE ME UP...!

SOMEHOW... I FELT LIKE I WAS GETTING SWALLOWED UP, SUCKED DOWN INTO THE DARK-NESS...
AND IT FELT LIKE... I WAS NEVER GONNA BE ABLE TO COME BACK...

KEITH... HE'S JUST LIKE TENMA...
THEY'RE BOTH POSSESSED BY THE EVIL GODS!

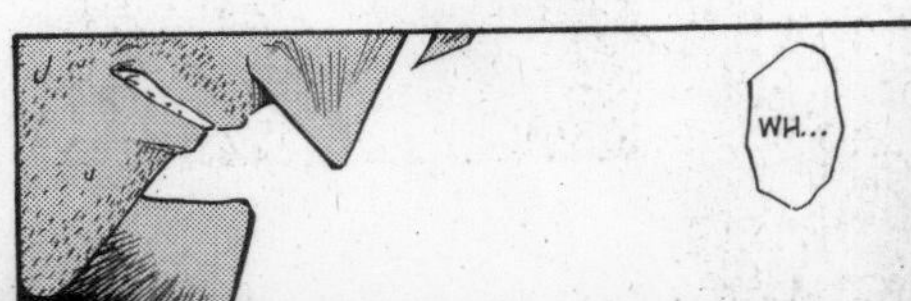

WH...

READ THIS WAY

WHY ...?
WHY... WON'T YOU... DIE?

...
I'M... DEAD... AND YOU'RE... STILL... ALIVE...
IT'S... NOT FAIR...

ZM
ZM
AM I...
AM I GONNA... DISAPPEAR... AGAIN? DOWN INTO... NOTHING... INTO BLACKNESS...
ZM
ZM

D-
D-
D-
TH... THI... THIS TIME...
JONO... UCHII...
ARE YOU GONNA... HUNT ME...ALL THE WAY INTO THE... JAWS OF DEATH...?
D-

KEITH...

IT'S MY TURN.
DON'T BE AFRAID, KEITH...
I'M... GOING TO SAVE YOU NOW!

I SUMMON GEARFRIED THE IRON KNIGHT!!
TAKE THIS HIT AND COME TO YOUR SENSES!
JONOUCHI...!!
BOOM
GEARFRIED ATK 1800
FIENDISH ENGINE Ω ATK 700

THUKK
KKK
OM
UNGH ...!
STAGGER

BAM
IT'S OVER, KEITH.
THUD

UNLIKE THOSE FREAKY SHADOW GAMES, YOU DON'T FEEL PAIN FROM SOLID VISION DUELS.
BUT IF YOU'RE A DUELIST, YOU MUST'VE FELT THAT ONE!
HUH ...?

THAT'S PROOF YOU'RE ALIVE AS A DUELIST!

KLIK
...

FWIP
WHAK

NOT... YET...

FIGHT ME...ONE MORE TIME...!
ONE MORE... TIME...

...
NOPE. NOT A CHANCE.

PUT ON... THAT BLACK DUEL DISK...
THERE...

I'M NOT GONNA DUEL YOU WHEN YOU'RE LIKE THIS.

THUD

Y...
YOU LITTLE...

RIGHT NOW, YOU'RE LIKE...LIKE SOME DEMON OF VENGEANCE.
BUT EVEN *YOU* MUST'VE BEEN DIFFERENT THE FIRST TIME YOU PICKED UP A CARD...

BACK WHEN YOU DUELED JUST FOR THE FUN OF IT...

HEH... MAN, I CAN'T IMAGINE YOU EVER BEING LIKE THAT...

...
I'M GIVING THIS BACK TO YOU.

TIME MACHINE
(TRAP CARD)

USE THAT CARD, REMEMBER HOW IT FEELS TO DUEL FOR FUN AND THEN COME FIND ME.

FACE ME AS A DUELIST INSTEAD OF A DEMON...
...AND I'LL DUEL YOU ANYTIME YOU WANT!

GO TO THE LAST ROUND...!

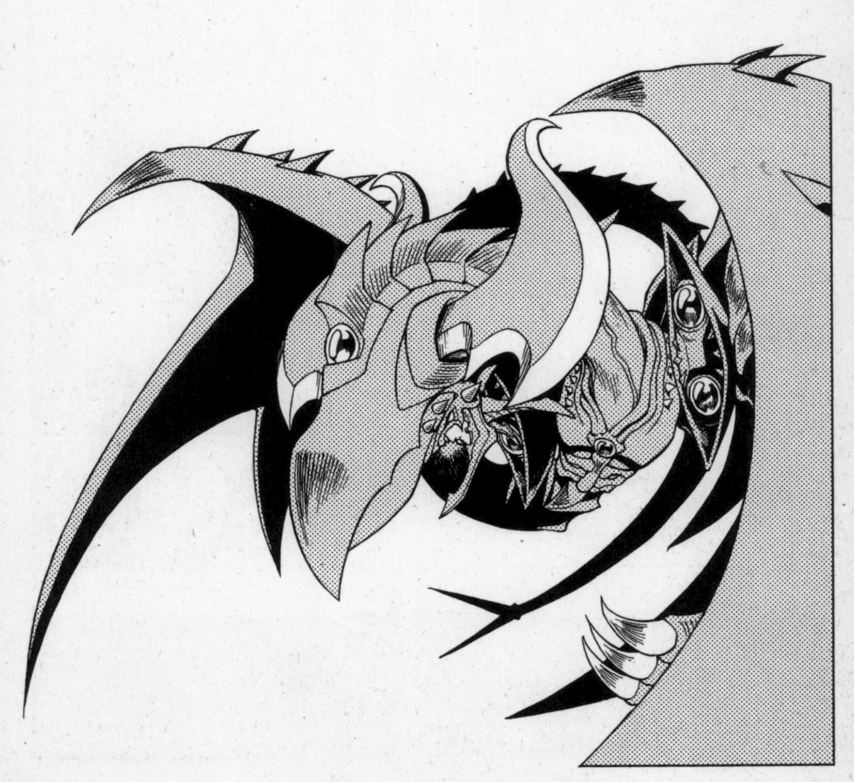

Duel Round 37: The Final Showdown

ANZU...

VREEEN

HEY, HONDA! THERE YOU ARE!
TMP TMP
JONO-UCHI!
!!

DID YOU WIN?!

OF COURSE!

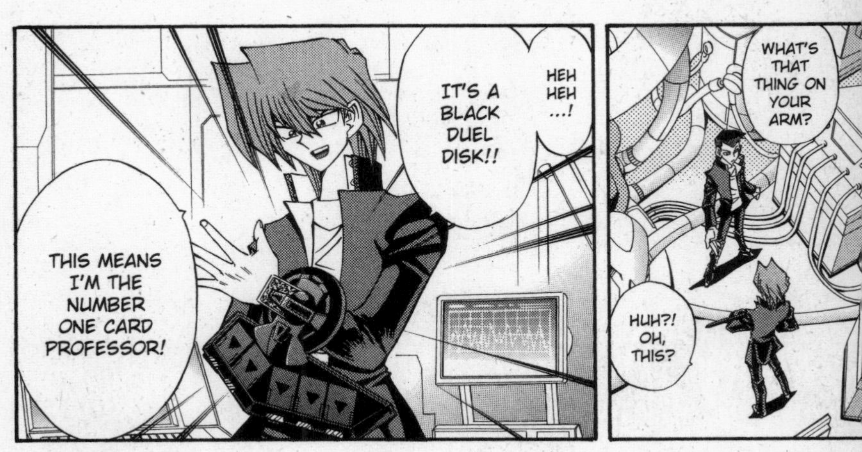

WHAT'S THAT THING ON YOUR ARM?
HUH?! OH, THIS?
HEH HEH ...!
IT'S A BLACK DUEL DISK!!
THIS MEANS I'M THE NUMBER ONE CARD PROFESSOR!

YOU'RE THE TOP CARD PROFESSOR...?!
MAN, THEY'RE JUST GIVING THOSE AWAY THESE DAYS...
HEY, NO NEED TO GET HARSH...

READ
THIS
WAY

FORGET ABOUT THAT!
LOOK AT THIS! ANZU'S STILL CONNECTED TO THIS THING!

SO SHE REALLY WAS TOO HEAVY FOR YOU TO CARRY, HUH?
AS IF!

ALL RIGHT!! LET'S GET HER OUTTA HERE!
THIS MACHINE'S IN THE WAY...
WAUGH !!
WAIT WAIT WAIT!

HE'S RIGHT, JONOUCHI.
YOU CAN'T TAKE ANZU OUT OF THERE YET.

SHE'S STILL LINKED IN TO THE EVIL GOD CARDS.
ANZU'S SPIRIT HAS BECOME DETACHED...

UNLESS WE CUT THE LINK TO THE EVIL GODS...
...ANZU'S SPIRIT WILL NEVER RETURN TO HER BODY!

OF ALL THE STUPID—!! YOU MEAN SHE'S RIGHT HERE, BUT WE CAN'T SAVE HER?!
WHAM

THERE'S JUST ONE WAY.
WE HAVE TO RENDER THE EVIL GODS POWER-LESS...

YOU MEAN...
DEFEAT THE EVIL GOD CARDS?!
YUGI ...!!

Duel Round 37: The Final Showdown

YAKO !!

DDO

SHM

KAIBA... ARE YOU ALL RIGHT?

ARE YOU ACTUALLY *WORRIED* ABOUT ME?
I MUST REALLY BE LOSING MY TOUCH.

RGH ...

HMPH ...
I WAS EXPOSED TO THE POISON OF THE SO-CALLED EVIL GODS... THAT'S ALL.

THE FACT THAT YOU MADE IT UP HERE...
...MEANS THAT NONE OF THE CARD PROFESSORS COULD STOP YOU.

I'M NOT SURPRISED.
AFTER ALL, ONLY I CAN DEFEAT YOU!

KAIBA...

YAKO ...

WHAT ARE YOU DOING HERE...
...GEKKO ...?

YAKO ...
THE REBIRTH OF AVATAR PROJECT HAS FAILED.

LET'S END THIS...

...
YOU'RE TELLING ME TO END IT...?

WHO DO YOU THINK YOU'RE TALKING TO, GEKKO?

FAILED ?!
THOOM

OF COURSE IT FAILED!
BECAUSE OF THOSE TWO!

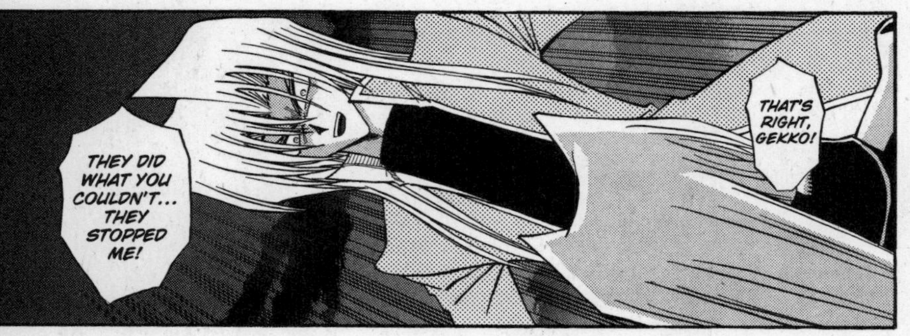
THAT'S RIGHT, GEKKO!
THEY DID WHAT YOU COULDN'T... THEY STOPPED ME!

HEH HEH HEH...
ALL YOU DID WAS WHAT I ORDERED YOU TO... POSSESSED BY THE POWER OF THE EVIL GODS!
HYA HA HA HA HA ...!
YOU'RE RIGHT, YAKO...
I LOST. I'M POWER-LESS...

I CAN'T FIGHT YOU ANYMORE... BUT *HE* CAN.

HEH HEH...
NOT ONLY DID HE BEAT YOU, YOU'VE GIVEN UP!
HOW THE "PERFECT DUELIST" HAS FALLEN.

A PERFECT DUELIST.
YES... MASTER PEGASUS CALLED ME THAT...

IT MADE ME SO PROUD...
BUT OVER THE COURSE OF MANY DUELS...

...I REALIZED SOME-THING.

MASTER PEGASUS NEVER MEANT THAT I WAS *THE* PERFECT DUELIST.
WHAT ...?!
D D D D
WHEN WE WERE WITH MASTER PEGASUS, I DID WIN MY DUELS WITH YOU AND THE OTHER PEGASUS PRODIGIES. BY A SMALL MARGIN.
BUT EVERY TIME WE DUELED, THE DIFFERENCE IN OUR DUELIST LEVELS DIMINISHED.
I COULDN'T HELP BUT REALIZE... MY OPPONENTS WERE GETTING BETTER.
...
BOBOMP

I THINK MASTER PEGASUS MUST HAVE SEEN WITH HIS MILLENNIUM EYE...
...THAT MY DUELIST LEVEL WAS AS HIGH AS IT WOULD EVER BE...
WHAT...
THM
THM
THM
...ARE YOU SAYING ...?
I AM "PERFECTED." I WILL NEVER GROW.
GRAB
GEKKO ...!!

IN FACT... I THINK THE ONE HE SAW POTENTIAL IN, THE ONE HE THOUGHT WOULD BECOME A FIRST-RATE DUELIST...
...WAS YOU, YAKO!
B'BMP
...
D...
SHOVE
DON'T YOU DARE SAY THAT TO ME!
DON'T TELL ME THAT, GEKKO!

GEKKO ...!
...
• "GEKKO" MEANS "MOONLIGHT" IN JAPANESE.
DO YOU KNOW HOW I FEEL WHEN YOU SAY THAT?!
YOU'RE JUST LIKE YOUR NAME! YOU'RE LIKE THE MOON!
MASTER PEGASUS WAS THE SUN, AND YOU WERE A REFLECTION OF HIM!
AND I'M LEFT TO CRAWL THROUGH THE DARKNESS...
CRAWLING BLINDLY... SEARCHING FOR LIGHT...

I WILL GET MY LIGHT. THE R.A. PROJECT ISN'T DEAD YET...

I STILL HAVE THE VESSEL, ANZU MAZAKI...

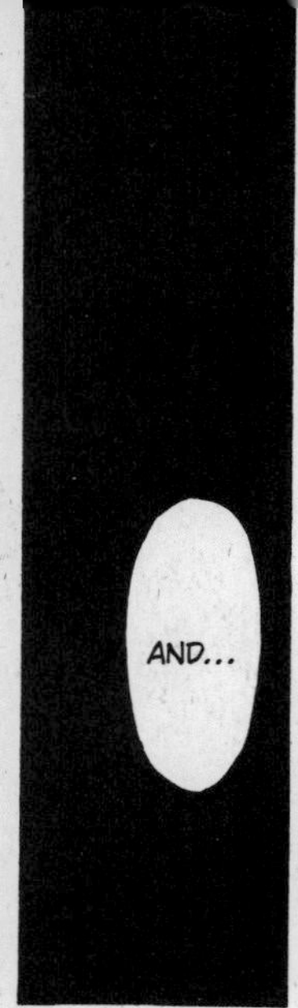
AND...

I HAVE YOU, YUGI MUTOU! THE ONE I HATE!

BAM

YOU HOUNDED MASTER PEGASUS TO DEATH!
!!
WHEN I CRUSH YOU, THE WAY WILL BE CLEARED FOR HIS RESURRECTION!
YAKO, WAIT!
WHAT KEITH HOWARD TOLD YOU ABOUT YUGI KILLING MASTER PEGASUS...
IT WAS A LIE!
NO, IT WASN'T.
YUGI MUTOU DEFEATED MASTER PEGASUS AT DUELIST KINGDOM.

AND THEN MASTER PEGASUS...
...VOLUNTARILY ACCEPTED DEATH.

WHAT ...?!
...
THERE'S NO WAY THAT SOMEONE AS POWERFUL AS MASTER PEGASUS COULD HAVE DIED UNLESS HE WANTED TO.

...
IT DOESN'T MATTER NOW WHO ACTUALLY PERFORMED THE DEED.

YAKO ...
SHF
YUGI...

EVEN SO...
MY FIGHT WITH PEGASUS WAS A BATTLE BETWEEN TWO DUELISTS!

RELEASE ANZU!
OUR FIGHT HAS NOTHING TO DO WITH HER!

THAT'S NO LONGER POSSIBLE...
WHAT ...?!

ANZU MAZAKI HAS BECOME PART OF THE EVIL GODS. SHE IS BUILT INTO THE DUEL RING SERVER...
DRAG HER OUT OF IT, AND SHE WILL DIE.

RRGH ...!

HEH HEH...
DO YOU LIKE IT? THE DIVINE PUNISHMENT OF THE EVIL GODS?!
ZM
ZM ZM
SHF

READ THIS WAY

COME AT ME, YUGI!!
G
G
YOU ASKED FOR IT!
G
G
G

THIS IS IT! THE FINAL SHOW-DOWN!!

GWOO OO OO O

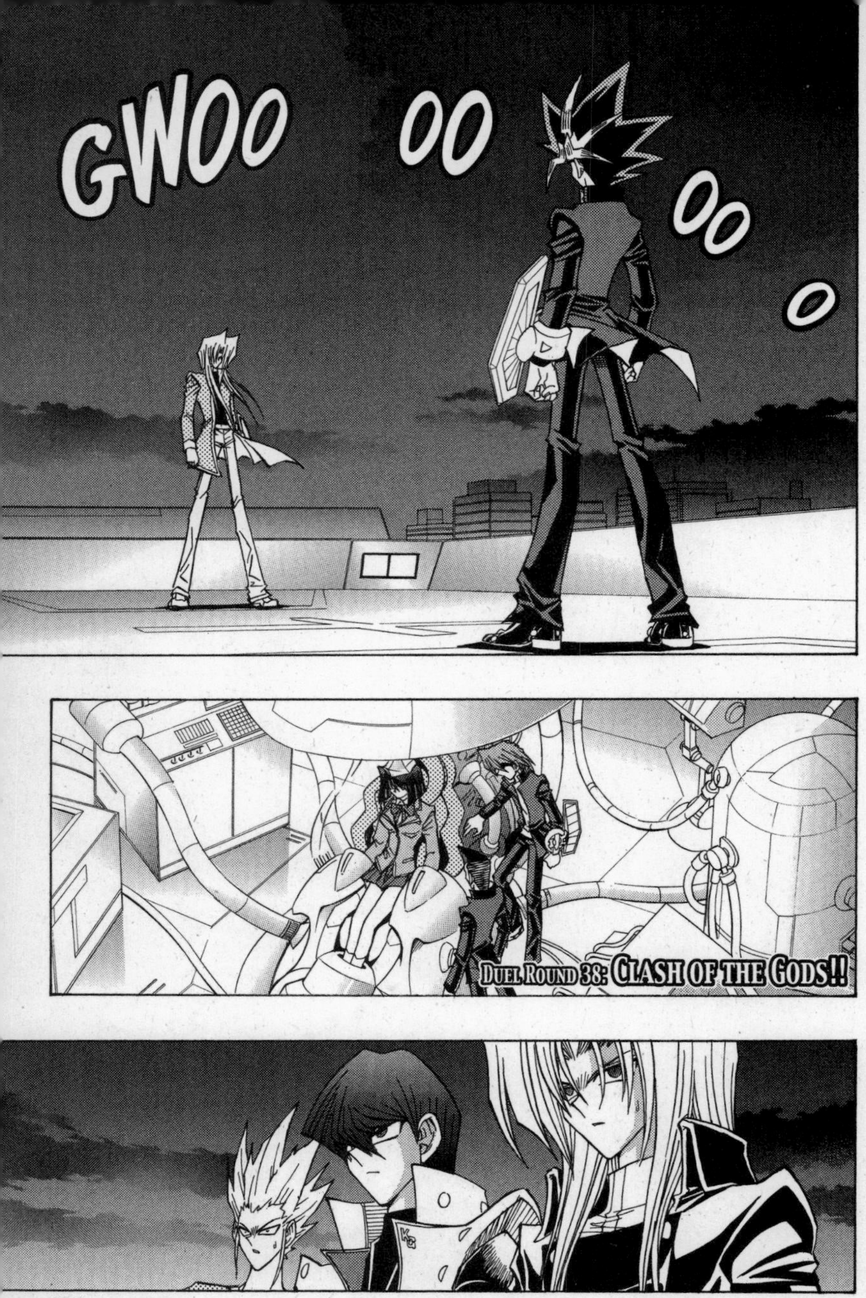

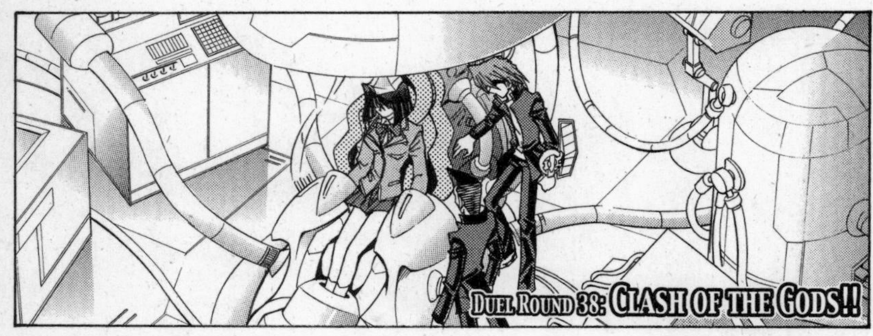
DUEL ROUND 38: CLASH OF THE GODS!!

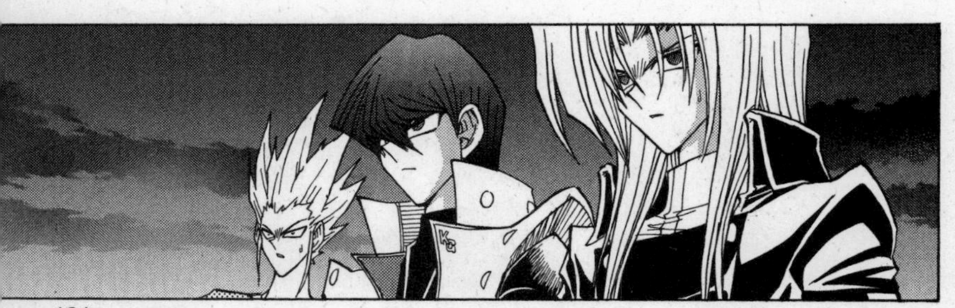

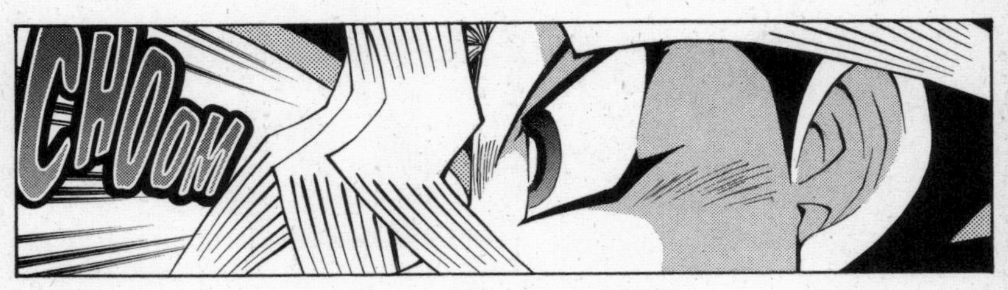

BANG

LET'S DUEL!!!

Duel Round 38: Clash of the Gods!!

HERE I GO, YAKO!!
BRING IT, YUGI...!
THE FIRST TURN IS MINE!
YUGI MUTOU
Life Points 4000
I PLAY ALPHA THE MAGNET WARRIOR IN DEFENSE MODE!
ALPHA THE MAGNET WARRIOR
Alpha, Beta, and Gamma meld as one to form a powerful monster.
ATK/1400 DEF/1700
I ALSO SET ONE CARD FACE DOWN!!

THAT ENDS MY TURN!

MY TURN!
YAKO TENMA
Life Points 4000

I DRAW!
!!
HEH HEH...

I SET ONE CARD FACE DOWN ON THE FIELD...
BANG

...AND SUMMON THIS MONSTER!!

BEAST KING BARBAROS!!!
D...D...D...D...
Beast King Barbaros
★★★★★★★★
You can Normal Summon or Set this card without Tributing. If you do, its original ATK becomes 1900. You can Tribute 3 monsters to Tribute Summon this card. When you do, destroy all cards your opponent controls.
ATK 3000 DEF 1200
DID HE...JUST SUMMON AN EIGHT-STAR MONSTER WITHOUT SACRIFICING?!
BARBAROS IS THE GREATEST OF THE DEMIGODS, THE HEAVENLY SERVANTS OF THE GODS!
AN EIGHT-STAR MONSTER THAT CAN BE SUMMONED WITHOUT SACRIFICES!
HOWEVER, WITHOUT SACRIFICES, ITS ATTACK POWER IS LOWERED TO 1900...
BEAST KING BARBAROS
ATK 1900

TORNADO SHAPER!!
BUT EVEN AT 1900 ATTACK POINTS ...
...HE'S STRONG ENOUGH TO DEFEAT YOUR MONSTER, YUGI!
RRGH ...
VERY WELL!
REVERSE CARD, OPEN!!

SOUL ROPE!
I PAY 1000 LIFE POINTS...
SHWO
...AND SUMMON KING'S KNIGHT!!
Soul Rope
(TRAP CARD)
Activate only by paying 1000 Life Points when a monster you control is destroyed and sent to the Graveyard. Special Summon 1 Level 4 monster from your Deck.
NOW IT'S MY TURN!
YUGI MUTOU
Life Points 3000
!!
BAM
I SUMMON QUEEN'S KNIGHT!!
AND SINCE THE KING AND QUEEN ARE ON THE FIELD TOGETHER...

THEY CALL FORTH JACK'S KNIGHT!!
THE FACE CARD WARRIORS ARE SUMMONED!
DOOM
WHAT SPEED! YUGI'S ALREADY GOT THE THREE SACRIFICES THAT HE NEEDS TO SUMMON A GOD!
...
BUT THOSE PLAYING CARD SWORDSMEN CAN'T DEFEAT BARBAROS...
AND NOW ...

I PLAY ONE CARD FACE DOWN...
...AND END MY TURN!!
BAMM

KING, JACK AND QUEEN...
THREE FACE CARD SWORDS-MEN TO CALL DOWN A GOD, HMM...?

BUT NOT IF MY BEAST KING KILLS THEM FIRST!

IF EVEN ONE OF YOUR THREE SWORDSMEN IS LOST, YOU CAN'T SUMMON A GOD ON YOUR NEXT TURN!

HERE I GO! BATTLE PHASE!!

BEAST KING BARBAROS ATTACKS!!
HEH HEH...
DON'T FEAR THE GODS, YAKO!
FACE DOWN CARD, REVEAL!
POLYMERIZATION
(SPELL CARD)
WHAT?!
THREE FACE CARD SWORDS-MEN, BECOME ONE!
GWRRRRR

SHNN
ZNNNK
THE IMPERIAL KNIGHT...
ARCANA KNIGHT JOKER !!!!
DOOOM
ARCANA KNIGHT JOKER
ATK 3800

WHROOO
NGH ...!
SH
YAKO TENMA
Life Points 2100

ARCANA KNIGHT JOKER, WITH 3800 ATTACK POINTS!
THAT MOVE JUST PUT YUGI IN THE LEAD...!

YUGI...
SO YOU GAVE UP ON SUMMONING A GOD AND LEFT THE FIELD TO A FUSION MONSTER...

BUT...YAKO'S DECK IS SPECIALLY DESIGNED FOR SUMMONING THE EVIL GODS AT HIGH SPEED.
JUST HOW MANY TURNS WILL YOU BE ABLE TO LAST WITH THAT MONSTER...?

FWOOOOOO
YUGI ...

OOOOOO
I THINK YOU SAID, "DON'T FEAR THE GODS"?

IT'S YOU WHO SHOULD BE AFRAID.

TREMBLE AT THE PULSE OF THE EVIL GOD!

FACE-DOWN TRAP CARD, REVEAL!

LEVEL RESIST WALL!

LEVEL RESIST WALL
(TRAP CARD)

Activate only when a monster you control is destroyed and sent to the Graveyard. Special Summon Monster Card(s) from your hand whose total Level Stars exactly equal the Level of the destroyed monster.

THIS CARD ALLOWS ME TO SPECIAL SUMMON MONSTERS UNTIL THEIR COMBINED STAR LEVEL EQUALS THAT OF BEAST KING BARBAROS WHOM YOU DESTROYED!

THOOM

THOOM

THOOM

THOOM

ANGEL 01
ATK 200 DEF 300

CASSIMOLAR
ATK 1000 DEF 1200

LERAJE THE GOD OF ARCHERY
ATK 1800 DEF 1600

HE SUMMONED THREE MONSTERS IN AN INSTANT...!

TSK TSK... I'M NOT DONE YET! I ALSO GET TO SUMMON A NORMAL MONSTER ON THIS TURN!

WHAT ?!
FOR MY FOURTH MONSTER...

I SUMMON VOTIS IN DEFENSE MODE!!
VOTIS
ATK 1700 DEF 1900
ALL RIGHT! MY TURN IS OVER!

...

YAKO'S IMPRESSIVE. I CAN'T BELIEVE HE MANAGED TO SUMMON FOUR MONSTERS IN JUST ONE TURN...
AND NOW, IF HE HAS A GOD CARD IN HIS HAND...

...

MY TURN...

ZM
ZM
ZM
ZM

ARCANA KNIGHT JOKER ATTACKS !!

VOTIS DIES!

FSSHHH

HEH HEH HEH ...
IS THAT ALL YOU'VE GOT? I STILL HAVE THREE MONSTERS LEFT...
ZM
ZM
ZM

I PLAY ONE CARD FACE DOWN AND END MY TURN.

HEH HEH... YEH...
YEH HEE...

YAA HA HA HA HA HA HA!

YAKO'S STILL GOT THREE MONSTERS ON THE FIELD...
...AND NOW IT'S HIS TURN.

IS THIS IT...?

HA HA HA HA HA! IT'S MY TURN!

BAM

ACCEPT THE BLOOD OF THE DEMIGODS! CONSUME THE SACRIFICE, AND BECOME FLESH!

GWRRRR

THE WICKED ERASER!!!

DWOOOOOOO
THE WICKED...
...ERASER...
THERE... THERE IT IS...!
THE DARK GOD BROUGHT FORTH BY YAKO'S SPIRIT...
SO THIS IS THE THIRD EVIL GOD...
THE ERASER!!

THE ERASER'S ATTACK POINTS ARE EQUAL TO THE NUMBER OF CARDS ON MY OPPONENT'S FIELD, TIMES 1000!
THE WICKED ERASER
This card cannot be Special Summoned. This card cannot be Normal Summoned or Set except by Tributing 3 monsters. The ATK and DEF of this card are each equal to the number of cards your opponent controls x 1000. When this card is destroyed and sent to the Graveyard, destroy all cards on the field. During your Main Phase, you can destroy this card.
ATK ? DEF ?
ON YOUR FIELD, RIGHT NOW...
!
...YOU HAVE THE JACK, KING AND QUEEN CARDS WHICH MAKE UP YOUR FUSION MONSTER, PLUS ONE FACE-DOWN CARD!
FOUR CARDS IN ALL!!
DIGESTIVE BREATH!!!
SHH

THAT MEANS THE ERASER'S ATTACK POWER IS 4000!
HA HA HA HA HA!
ALL I NEED TO DO IS BREATHE TO KILL YOU!
THE WICKED ERASER
ATK 4000
GWAAAH!
YOUR HOPES ARE MELTING AWAY...
YUGI...

Duel Round 39: Speed Summon!!

RRGH ...!
TH... THIS IS...

THE WICKED ERASER!!
DUEL ROUND 39: SPEED SUMMON!!

SHOOOO

GEKKO ...
IS THAT YAKO'S THIRD GOD?

THE WICKED ERASER...
ITS ATTACK POWER IS DETERMINED BY THE NUMBER OF CARDS ON THE OTHER PLAYER'S FIELD.

FOR A GOD, IT ISN'T VERY SELF-SUFFICIENT...

HMPH!
I KNEW IT. IT'S NOTHING MORE THAN A FALSE GOD!

...

YAKO...

I SET ONE CARD FACE DOWN ON THE FIELD.
TURN OVER!
BAM
YUGI MUTOU
Life Points 2800
YAKO TENMA
Life Points 2100

SO THIS... IS THE WICKED ERASER...

RIGHT NOW, ALL I HAVE ON MY FIELD IS A SINGLE FACE-DOWN CARD...
MY TURN...

IF I PUT A MONSTER CARD ON THE FIELD...
...THE ERASER'S ATTACK POWER WILL JUMP TO 2000!

IN THAT CASE...
...I'LL USE THIS!

BIG SHIELD GARDNA, IN DEFENSE MODE!

BA

NG

BIG SHIELD GARDNA
★★★★
ATK 100 DEF 2600

D-D-D-

RIGHT NOW, YOUR ERASER HAS 2000 ATTACK POINTS!

THAT MEANS YOUR EVIL GOD CAN'T BREAK THROUGH THIS SHIELD!

YOU MUST BE SO PLEASED WITH YOURSELF. STOPPING A GOD WITH A FOUR-STAR MONSTER... DO YOU REALLY THINK THAT'LL WORK?
WHAT?!

THE WICKED ERASER...

...IS A BEING THAT ERASES EVERY-THING...

...EVEN OTHER GODS!

YOU THINK YOU CAN DEFEAT THE ERASER...

...BUT I'LL ERASE YOUR ARROGANCE INSTEAD!

ARRO-GANCE ...?!

IS IT MY TURN YET?

WATCH THIS, YUGI...

WHAT ...?!
N...NO WAY!
HE'S SACRIFICING HIS OWN GOD?!
I SACRIFICE THE ERASER!!
YA HA HA HA HA HA!

SHGOOOOOOO

WHEN THE WICKED ERASER GOES TO THE GRAVEYARD...
...IT TAKES ALL THE CARDS ON THE FIELD ALONG WITH IT!!

MY FACE-DOWN CARD! BIG SHIELD GARDNA!
THEY'RE VANISHING...!!
OOOOOOOO

GWOOOOOOOO

WHAT'S THIS ...?!
ZUM ZUM
I SUMMON GAAP THE DIVINE SOLDIER!
DOOOOM
GAAP THE DIVINE SOLDIER
★★★★★★
Once per turn, you can reveal any number of God-Type monsters in your hand to give this card 300 ATK for each revealed card, until the End Phase.
ATK 2200 DEF 2000

READ THIS WAY

GAAP IS A SIX-STAR MONSTER! HE USED THE EVIL GOD AS A SACRIFICE TO SUMMON THAT...?!

AND... THANKS TO THE ERASER'S EFFECT...
...YUGI'S FIELD IS COMPLETELY EMPTY...

GAAP'S ATTACK CAN'T FAIL TO GET THROUGH ...!

YEH HEH HEH...
IN ADDITION TO THAT, IF I EXPOSE THE GOD-TYPE CARDS IN MY HAND TO MY OPPONENT, THE WAR GOD'S ATTACK POWER IS BOOSTED!

!!

LET'S SEE... IT LOOKS AS THOUGH THE ONLY GOD-MONSTER IN MY HAND NOW...
...IS THIS ONE...

THE WICKED AVATAR
B-BMP
TH...THE WICKED AVATAR!!
HE ALREADY... HAD IT IN HIS HAND!
MY AVATAR GIVES GAAP STRENGTH!
GAAP THE DIVINE SOLDIER ATK 2500

READ THIS WAY

FUR-
THER
MORE
...
...I SET
ONE
MORE
CARD
FACE
DOWN.
BAM

HEH
HEH
HEH...
MY GOD
WILL GUIDE
GAAP
STRAIGHT
TO YOU...
ITS AIM IS
UNERRING...

RRGH...!
HERE I
COME,
YUGI!!
WAR GOD
GAAP!
DIRECT
ATTACK
ON THE
PLAYER!

GWAAGH...!!!
YUGI MUTOU
Life Points 300
HYA HA HA HA HA HA HA!
FSSSHH

BANG

A CARD ON YUGI'S FIELD ...?!

HOW ...?!

ALL YOUR FACE-DOWN CARDS SHOULD HAVE BEEN ERASED...

CROSS COUNTER TRAP

(TRAP SPELL CARD)

During the turn this card is sent from the field to the Graveyard by the effect of your opponent's card, you can activate 1 Spell or Trap Card from your hand.

THIS IS THE CARD THAT WAS SENT TO THE GRAVEYARD BY ERASER'S EFFECT!

CROSS COUNTER TRAP!

WHEN THIS CARD IS SENT TO THE GRAVEYARD, IT ALLOWS ME TO PLAY ANOTHER CARD FROM MY HAND!
NOW THAT I'VE SUSTAINED A DIRECT ATTACK...
...THE CARD I'M ACTIVATING IS...

DOOM

STAIRWAY TO THE UNDERWORLD!

STAIRWAY TO THE UNDERWORLD

(TRAP SPELL CARD)

Activate only when you take Battle Damage to your Life Points from a direct attack, and you do not control any monster on your side of the field. Special Summon 1 each of "Messenger of Hades - Gorz" and "Messenger of Hades - Kaien" from your Deck to your side of the field.

THE DARK ONES!!!
THE EMISSARIES! GORZ AND KAIEN!!!
Kaien the Emissary of Darkness
Gorz the Emissary of Darkness
ATK 2700 DEF 2500

A SECOND AGO... HE'D LOST EVERY-THING...

...AND NOW HE'S SUMMONED TWO SEVEN-STAR MONSTERS ...?!

D- D- D-

FWOOOOO

OOOO

SO THIS... IS THE DUELIST WHO DEFEATED MASTER PEGASUS...

I KNEW YUGI COULD DO IT.

BUT HE'S ONLY CLOSED THE GAP...
YAKO'S STILL ON EQUAL FOOTING WITH HIM...

NOT BAD ...
YUGI TOOK A BAD HIT, BUT HE SURVIVED...
...AND NOW HE'S TAKEN THE LEAD WITH TWO SEVEN-STAR MONSTERS ...

BUT...

LURKING IN YAKO'S HAND...
...IS YET ANOTHER EVIL GOD!

IT'S...
...MY TURN.

ZM
ZM
ZM

EVEN SO...

THE EVIL GODS ARE TEN-STAR MONSTERS. TO SUMMON ONE...
...HE'LL NEED THREE MONSTERS TO USE AS SACRIFICES...
BAM
I SET ONE CARD FACE DOWN!

ZM ZM ZM ZM

IS THIS IT...?

I HAVE TO KEEP HIM FROM SUMMONING THE AVATAR!

HERE I COME, YAKO!!

GORZ THE EMISSARY OF DARKNESS, ATTACK!!

SLAY GAAP THE DIVINE SOLDIER!

SKA

RRGH ...!
YAKO TENMA
Life Points 1900
NOW FOR A DIRECT ATTACK BY KAIEN!!
WHAT ?!
REVERSE CARD, OPEN!
BAM
TRAP CARD! YELLOW ALERT!
YELLOW ALERT
(TRAP CARD)
Activate only when your opponent declares an attack. Special Summon 1 monster from your hand and it will become the target of the attack. At the end of the Battle Phase, the Summoned monster is returned to its owner's hand.
I SPECIAL SUMMON A MONSTER FROM MY HAND TO SHIELD ME!
TELLUS THE LITTLE ANGEL, IN DEFENSE MODE!
BOOM

SLASHHH
TELLUS IS SPLIT IN HALF!
BUT... ALTHOUGH TELLUS IS DEAD, IT LEAVES A WING ON THE FIELD!
TELLUS THE LITTLE ANGEL
When this card is sent to the Graveyard, Special Summon 1 "Tellus Wing Token" (Fairy-Type/LIGHT/Level 1/ATK 0/DEF 0) to your side of the field.
ATK/500 DEF/500
IF HE'D USED YELLOW ALERT TO CALL OUT THE EVIL GOD, HE COULD HAVE TAKEN DOWN ONE OF THE EMISSARIES OF DARKNESS...
WHY DID HE USE TELLUS AS A SHIELD?
DOM
TELLUS' WING
ATK 0 DEF 0
HEH HEH HEH...
DO YOU HEAR IT?
THE PULSE OF THE JASHIN IS GETTING LOUDER...
?!
AND NOW, ON MY TURN...

FROM MY HAND...
I ACTIVATE THE SPELL CARD MULTIPLY !!
MULTIPLY
(SPELL CARD)
!!
TELLUS' WING TOKEN SPLIT INTO THREE...!
IT CAN'T BE...
TO THINK HE'D GET THREE SACRIFICES SO EASILY...!
AND NOW, YUGI... ANOTHER EVIL GOD WILL MANIFEST ITSELF BEFORE YOU!
LOOK AND DESPAIR...
HYA HA HA HA HA HA!

...AS I SUMMON THE WICKED AVATAR!!
THE WICKED AVATAR
This card cannot be Special Summoned. This card cannot be Normal Summoned or Set except by Tributing 3 monsters. Your opponent cannot activate Spell or Trap Cards until the end of their 2nd turn after this card is Normal Summoned. The ATK and DEF of this card are each 1 point higher than the highest ATK on the field (except "The Wicked Avatar").
ATK ? DEF ?

DOOOM
Duel Round 40: Reign of the Avatar
SHREEEEEE
THE DUEL RING SERVER HAS STARTED PERFORMING ALL KINDS OF STRANGE CALCULATIONS AGAIN!
EEEEE
THAT'S IMPOSSIBLE!
MY BIG BROTHER'S CODE SHOULD HAVE STOPPED ALL OF TENMA'S PROGRAMS ...!
EEEE

ROARRRR

DOES THIS MEAN IT CAN'T BE STOPPED ANYMORE?
NOT EVEN WITH MY BIG BROTHER'S PROGRAM-MING?

UNLESS ...
...SOME KIND OF VIRUS IS BEING UPLOADED FROM THE EVIL GOD CARDS THEMSELVES!

FLASHHH

WH...
WHAT'S THAT?!

SOMETHING'S WRONG WITH ANZU!
MMM
THE MACHINE'S STARTING UP AGAIN!
WMM
MM

ZZT
A... ANZU ?!
ZT
ZT

ANZU, WHAT'S THE MATTER?!!
ARE YOU OKAY ...?!
KZZT
ZZT

YEOW ...!

...
MAN...
ARE WE REALLY THAT HELPLESS ...?

ONLY ONE PERSON CAN FREE ANZU FROM THE EVIL GODS NOW...
GOOD LUCK, YUGI!

Duel Round 40: Reign of the Avatar

DO YOU SEE NOW?!
THIS IS MY EVIL GOD... MY OTHER SELF!
THE WICKED AVATAR!!
A JET-BLACK SUN, TWIN TO MY SUN GOD RA...
THE WICKED AVATAR...!!
THE ACCURSED GOD THAT STAINED YAKO'S SOUL BLACK...
SO HE FINALLY SUMMONED IT...
THE DARK GOD WHICH SURPASSES ALL OTHER MONSTERS...

COME! WICKED AVATAR!
TRANSFORM YOURSELF!!
!!
HYA HA HA HA HA! THE WICKED AVATAR TRANSCENDS EVERY OTHER MONSTER ON THE FIELD!
ITS REIGN IS ETERNAL!!
ZM
ZMM

DOOOMMM
A... ANZU?!
MMMMM
IN THE MIDST OF THE EVIL GOD'S VORTEX... FOR JUST A SECOND, I SAW ANZU!
IT LOOKS AS THOUGH YOUR PRECIOUS FRIEND IS ALREADY BEING ABSORBED BY THE EVIL GOD.
HEH HEH HEH...
WH... WHAT DID YOU SAY?!

SHE WILL BE DRUNK UP, EVERY LAST DROP...
THE WICKED AVATAR
ATK 2701
(Gorz the Emissary of Darkness Base)
UNLESS YOU CAN TOPPLE THIS EVIL GOD!!

YAKO... YOU PSYCHO-PATH!
YA HA HA HA HA HA!
THIS IS THE JUDGMENT OF THE AVATAR!
DEATH TO YOU AND THE ONES YOU LOVE!
D.D.D...
D
WICKED AVATAR! PUNISH HIM!

SLASH
KAIEN IS SPLIT IN TWO!
YUGI MUTOU
Life Points 99
RRGH ...!

YUGI!
THAT LAST ATTACK ...
...DROPPED YUGI DOWN TO 99 LIFE POINTS!
BAMM
I SET ONE CARD FACE DOWN...
...AND END MY TURN!
ZM
ZM
ZM
THE WICKED AVATAR...
ITS POWER IS UNSPEAKABLE...
IT TAKES THE ATTACK POWER OF THE STRONGEST MONSTER ON THE FIELD...
...AND SURPASSES IT BY JUST ONE POINT.

YUGI...
ARE YOU REALLY AS STRONG AS YOU THINK YOU ARE?
OR WILL THE AVATAR DESTROY YOUR GODS AND SCATTER THE PIECES?

WHAT'S WRONG, YUGI?
IT'S YOUR TURN!
...
FOR EVERY MOMENT YOU DELIBERATE, MORE OF ANZU'S SOUL IS ABSORBED...
SO MAKE IT FAST!
YOU SCUM...

IT'S MY TURN! DRAW!!!

I SEND ONE CARD FROM MY HAND TO THE GRAVE-YARD...

...AND SPECIAL SUMMON *THE TRICKY!!*

BA-DING

THE TRICKY

You can discard 1 card to Special Summon this card from your hand.

ATK 2000 DEF 1200

HA HA... TURNING TO DEFENSE, EH? TRYING TO STAY ALIVE ONE MORE TURN?
YOU'LL NEVER SAVE YOUR FRIEND ANZU THAT WAY...
NO!

ON THIS TURN...

!!
I'LL ATTACK THE EVIL GOD!
WHAT ?!
UNION ATTACK
(SPELL CARD)
Select 1 face-up monster you control. During the Battle Phase this turn, that monster gains ATK equal to the total ATK of all other face-up Attack Position monsters you control. This turn, that monster inflicts no Battle Damage to your opponent, and other face-up Attack Position monsters cannot attack.
I ACTIVATE THE SPELL CARD, UNION ATTACK!
D
M
OF COURSE! SINCE THE EVIL GOD'S ATTACK POWER IS BASED ON GORZ'S...
...IT'S STILL AT 2701...!
...USING THE COMBINED POWERS OF GORZ AND THE TRICKY!
WITH THIS CARD, I CAN DO 4700 POINTS OF DAMAGE TO THE EVIL GOD...

THE TRICKY AND GORZ ATTACK AS A TEAM!
KA
MAGIC SWORD BRUSH!!

SHOOOOOOOM
SHASH
SHNN
WHAT?!
GORZ WAS DEFEATED ?!
FSSHHHHH
BUT...
HOW?! THE EVIL GOD SHOULD HAVE BEEN THE ONE DESTROYED!

HEH HEH HEH...
I ACTIVATED MY FACE-DOWN CARD.

LOSS OF STRENGTH
(SPELL CARD)
Activate only during your Battle Phase. The ATK of 1 opponent's monster becomes 0. The monster may not declare an attack.
SPELL CARD! LOSS OF STRENGTH!

THIS CARD REDUCED THE TRICKY'S ATTACK POWER TO ZERO, ELIMINATING IT FROM THE BATTLE PHASE!

RGH ...!
ZM
ZM
ZM
THE TRICKY
ATK 0

THAT MEANS YOU ONLY DID 2700 POINTS OF DAMAGE TO THE AVATAR...
LOOKS LIKE YOU WERE JUST ONE POINT SHORT...
HEH HEH HEH...
THE WICKED AVATAR
ATK 1
(the Tricky Base)

I WENT OVER EVERY ONE OF YOUR DUELS IN THIS BUILDING.

FROM WHAT I SAW... THE ONLY CARD IN YOUR DECK CAPABLE OF CONQUERING THE JASHIN IS *UNION ATTACK!*

NOW THAT I'VE GOTTEN RID OF THAT CARD...
...THE EVIL GODS' REIGN IS UNSTOP-PABLE!
BAM

...

VERY WELL...
...I SET ONE CARD FACE DOWN...
BAM
...AND END MY TURN.
YUGI MUTOU
Life Points 98

MY TURN!

HEH HEH HEH... YUGI!
WHY DON'T WE THROW IN A LITTLE TWIST AT THE END?

WHAT ?!

FWIP
I ACTIVATE A SPELL CARD!!

FIEND'S SANCTUARY

(SPELL CARD)

Special Summon 1 "Metal Fiend Token." It cannot attack. When this Token battles, the opponent takes any Battle Damage its controller would have taken. Pay 1000 Life Points during each of your Standby Phases. If you do not, destroy the "Metal Fiend Token."

FIEND'S SANCTUARY!!

ZM

FIEND'S SANCTUARY SUMMONS A METAL DEVIL—EXCUSE ME, METAL FIEND—TO THE FIELD.

AND NOW, THAT FIEND WILL COPY YOU, YUGI!

ZM

ZM

METAL FIEND TOKEN
ATK 98

WH... WHAT THE ...?!

THE WICKED AVATAR IS CHANGING...

D.

D.

D.

D.

...INTO YUGI...?!

D.

FIEND'S SANCTUARY!!
FIEND'S SANCTUARY
(SPELL CARD)
Special Summon 1 "Metal Fiend Token." It cannot attack. When this Token battles, the opponent takes any Battle Damage its controller would have taken. Pay 1000 Life Points during each of your Standby Phases. If you do not, destroy the "Metal Fiend Token."
THE FIEND'S SANCTUARY CREATES A MAGIC PENTAGRAM...
...AND INSIDE THE PENTAGRAM APPEARS...
THE PENTAGRAM SUMMONS A METAL FIEND WITH A RATHER SPECIAL ABILITY...
IT BECOMES THE SAME ENTITY AS THE PLAYER IT REFLECTS!
DUEL ROUND 41: THE OTHER

Duel Round 41: The Other

ZM
HEH HEH...
ZM
ZM
ZM
P... PARTNER ...?!

G
G
THE METAL FIEND TOKEN HAS AN ATTACK POWER EQUAL TO THE LIFE POINTS OF THE PLAYER IT REFLECTS!
METAL FIEND
ATK 98
G
THE EVIL GOD TOOK...MY PARTNER'S SHAPE...

RRGH ...!
AND THE AVATAR TAKES THE FORM OF THE MOST POWERFUL MONSTER ON THE FIELD!
THE TRICKY
ATK 0

TAKE A GOOD LOOK, YUGI!!
THE WICKED AVATAR TOOK THE SHAPE OF THE METAL FIEND, WHICH IS SYNCHRONIZED WITH YOU!

AND ITS ATTACK POWER IS GREATER THAN YOUR LIFE POINTS!

THE WICKED AVATAR
ATK 99
(Yugi Mutou Base)

...

HOW DOES IT FEEL?! PREPARE TO KNOW DEFEAT AND DESPAIR...
...AT THE HANDS OF YOUR OTHER SELF!!

READ THIS WAY
YAKO... WHAT HAVE YOU DONE?!
ATTACKING WITH THE EVIL GOD WHEN IT LOOKS LIKE YUGI...
YUGI...
SUCCUMB TO YOUR SUPERIOR, YOU FOOL WITHOUT MEMORIES, YOU FOOL WHO DOESN'T EVEN KNOW HIS OWN FACE!
AVATAR! ATTACK!
MY...MY PARTNER IS ATTACKING ME...?!
S...
STOP!!

WH... WHAT THE...?!
SWORDS OF REVEALING LIGHT!!
SWORDS OF REVEALING LIGHT
(SPELL CARD)
Flip all monsters your opponent controls face-up. This card remains on the field for 3 of your opponent's turns. While this card is face-up on the field, monsters your opponent controls cannot declare an attack.
NGGH... THAT WAS MY FACE-DOWN SPELL CARD! SWORDS OF REVEALING LIGHT!
WHILE THIS IS ON THE FIELD, YOUR GOD CAN'T ATTACK FOR THREE TURNS!

HMPH...
SO, SINCE THE **SWORDS OF REVEALING LIGHT** AFFECT THE FIELD...
...EVEN THE EVIL GOD IS AFFECTED?

BUT YOU'RE RUNNING OUT OF CARDS. HOW LONG CAN YOU HOLD OUT?

WELL, WHO CARES?! I'LL SET TWO CARDS FACE DOWN...
BAM
BAM
...THEN END MY TURN!

...

MY TURN...
THE SWORDS WILL LAST FOR THREE MORE TURNS...
I HAVE TO REBUILD MY FORCES BEFORE THEY RUN OUT.
I DRAW.

AND THE CARD I DREW...

BAM

...IS THE SPELL CARD "MONSTER RECOVERY"!!

MONSTER RECOVERY
(SPELL CARD)

Take all of your own monsters on your side of the field and combine it with your Deck. At the same time combine your hand with your Deck and then shuffle it. Draw 5 cards from the Deck.

!!

THE TRICKY RETURNS TO MY DECK FROM THE FIELD. I SHUFFLE...

VWMMM

...AND DRAW A NEW FIVE-CARD HAND!

JUST WHAT I'D EXPECT FROM YUGI... HE DREW A GREAT CARD!

BUT...
NO MATTER WHAT SORT OF MONSTER HE HAS IN THAT NEW HAND, THE ODDS THAT IT CAN DEFEAT THE EVIL GOD ARE SLIM...

AND NOW...
...I SET TWO CARDS FACE DOWN ON THE FIELD!
BABAM

TURN OVER...

?!
HE DIDN'T SUMMON A MONSTER?!
DID HE NOT DRAW ONE...?!

YOU DIDN'T EVEN SUMMON A MONSTER TO ACT AS YOUR SHIELD...
DO THE **SWORDS OF REVEALING LIGHT** MAKE YOU FEEL THAT SAFE?

MY TURN!
I PAY 1000 LIFE POINTS...
...TO MAINTAIN THE METAL FIEND!
YAKO TENMA
Life Points 1900
↓
900

ZUM
ZUM
ZUM
ZUM

HE'S PAYING THE COST OF THE METAL FIEND EVEN THOUGH IT CAN'T ATTACK?!

HEH HEH HEH...
IF YOU THINK YOU HAVE THREE TURNS TO REST, THINK AGAIN.

BAM
I ACTIVATE DE-SPELL FROM MY HAND!!
DE-SPELL
(SPELL CARD)
Cancel the effect of any 1 Spell Card.
WHAT?!

THAT TAKES CARE OF **SWORDS OF REVEALING LIGHT!**

NOW... THE EVIL GOD IS ABLE TO ATTACK...

DID THAT SPOIL YOUR PLANS, YUGI?

TOO BAD. IT LOOKS LIKE THE EVIL GOD... I MEAN, YUGI MUTOU...

...WANTS TO CRUSH YOU SO BAD IT CAN'T WAIT!

!!

PREPARE TO FACE THE WRATH OF YOUR OWN AVATAR!
THE WRATH...
BAM
...OF THE OTHER YUGI WHO SECRETLY HATES YOU AND HAS YOUR SHAPE!
WH...
MY PARTNER... HATES ME?!

HMPH!
YOU LIVE IN HIS BODY, AND YOU DIDN'T NOTICE?

...

YOU AND THE OTHER YUGI...
YOU HAVE THE SAME FORM, BUT YOU AREN'T THE SAME...

READ THIS WAY

THE OTHER YUGI GAINED NOTHING.

YOU STOLE EVEN HIS CHANCES OF DOING SO!

THAT... THAT'S NOT...

EVEN ANZU MAZAKI... YOU'RE PLANNING TO TAKE HER TOO, AREN'T YOU?

REALLY! CAN ANYONE BLAME HIM FOR HIS ANGER?!

YA HA HA HA HA HA!

COULD IT BE TRUE...?

MASTER PEGASUS'S AFFECTION AND TRUST...
THE TITLE OF PERFECT DUELIST...
ALL OF THAT WENT TO GEKKO, MY DUPLICATE. I HATED GEKKO... LIKE YOU MUST HATE HIM...

HE'S... JUST LIKE ME...
HEH HEH HEH...

YAKO...

THE OTHER YUGI...

I'M... NOT ANGRY AT ALL.

BECAUSE ...
PARTNER...

THE OTHER ME...

...BROADENS MY OWN HORIZONS!

IT'S JUST NOT TRUE THAT I HAVEN'T GAINED ANYTHING BECAUSE OF THE OTHER ME.
?!

I'VE GAINED ALL SORTS OF IMPORTANT THINGS!

JONOUCHI AND HONDA...
...KAIBA ...
...AND ALL THE OTHER PEOPLE I MET THROUGH DUELS...

I WOULDN'T HAVE GAINED THOSE PRECIOUS FRIENDS...
...IF I DIDN'T HAVE MY OTHER SELF BESIDE ME!

IF I WERE ALONE, NO MATTER HOW I WISHED, THOSE THINGS WOULDN'T COME TRUE.
BUT...THE OTHER ME OPENED UP ALL SORTS OF POSSIBILITIES!

SO THAT EVIL GOD'S WRATH...
...ISN'T MINE!

IT'S YOURS, YAKO!

!!

YUGI... WHY?
YOU AND I ARE IN THE SAME POSITION... I THOUGHT YOU WOULD UNDERSTAND ME.

HOW CAN YOU BE OKAY WITH IT...?

HEH ...
HEH HEH ...

YOU REALLY ARE TOO DENSE.
I'M ALMOST JEALOUS...

YAKO...

I SUPPOSE YOU'RE RIGHT... PHYSICALLY, THERE'S ONLY ONE OF YOU.
YOU DON'T HAVE A LIVING, BREATHING REMINDER OF YOUR FAILURES AND WEAKNESSES THE WAY I DO!

ONE PERSON OR TWO, I'LL DEFEAT YOU TOGETHER!
BAM

TREMBLE BEFORE THE EVIL GOD, THE PERSONIFICATION OF MY WRATH!
GIVE UP AND LET ME KILL YOU!
HERE I COME! BATTLE PHASE!!

...THEN I'LL DESTROY IT AND FREE YOU!

BRING IT ON!

DOOOM

Duel Round 42: God vs. Evil God!!

RMMMMB

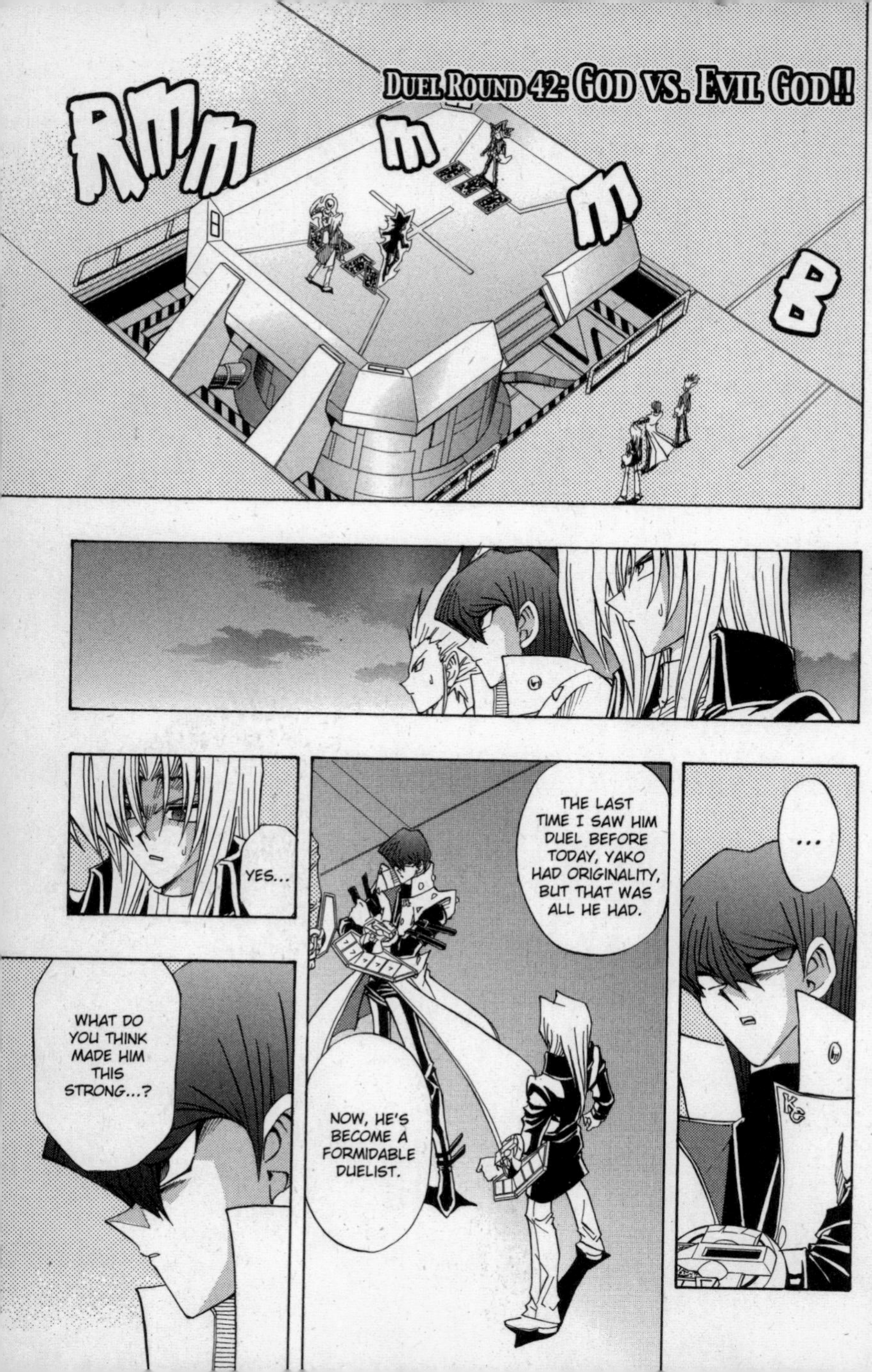

THE LAST TIME I SAW HIM DUEL BEFORE TODAY, YAKO HAD ORIGINALITY, BUT THAT WAS ALL HE HAD.
NOW, HE'S BECOME A FORMIDABLE DUELIST.

YES...

WHAT DO YOU THINK MADE HIM THIS STRONG...?

IT SEEMS AS THOUGH THE EVIL GODS WERE NOTHING MORE THAN THE TRIGGER.

HIS POWER IS BASED ON RAGE...
...BECAUSE OF HIS FEELINGS OF INFERIORITY TOWARD YOU!

INFERIORITY...

...!
I DON'T KNOW WHETHER THAT...
...SHOULD MAKE YOU HAPPY OR SAD...

I...

DUEL ROUND 42:
GOD VS.
EVIL GOD!!

YUGI!! SINK INTO DEEPEST DARKNESS!!

LET'S DUEL!!

BRING IT, YAKO!

THE EVIL GOD YUGI MOUNTS A DIRECT ATTACK!

GO!

DASH

READ THIS WAY
IF THIS ATTACK GETS THROUGH...
...I'LL BE THE WORLD'S GREATEST DUELIST!
I'M NOT BEATEN YET!
REVERSE CARD, OPEN!
THIS TRAP CARD, SHADOW GUARDSMEN...
...SUMMONS TWO GUARD TOKENS IN DEFENSE MODE!
SHADOW GUARDSMEN
(TRAP CARD)
Activate only during your opponent's Battle Phase. Special Summon 1 "Guard Token" (Warrior-Type/DARK/Level 1/ATK 1/DEF 1) for each monster your opponent controls. At the end of the Battle Phase, destroy any Token(s) Summoned by this card's effect.
GUARD TOKEN
ATK 1 DEF 1

THOOM

THOOM

THE GUARD TOKENS STOP ALL DAMAGE FROM THE ATTACK! I'M NOT HURT AT ALL!

NO! WAIT ...!

GASP

IT'S USELESS!

YOU CAN'T STOP THE EVIL GOD WITH THAT STUPID CARD!

FACE-DOWN CARD, REVEAL!

BERSERK MODE!

BAM

BAM

BAM

BERSERK MODE
(SPELL CARD)

During this turn's Battle Phase, all face-up monsters on the field are switched to Attack Position. In addition, all monsters on your side of the field must attack if possible.

THIS IS...!!

YOUR GUARD TOKENS SWITCH TO ATTACK POSITION!

READ THIS WAY

AND DON'T EVEN THINK ABOUT USING SOME FACE-DOWN CARD...
...TO UNDO MY CARD, SAVE YOUR GUARD TOKENS AND RUN AWAY!
YOU **WILL** DIE ON THIS TURN!
HEH ...

DON'T WORRY. I WON'T RUN AWAY FROM THIS BATTLE.

I KNOW WHAT YOU'RE UP TO, YUGI...!

GEKKO! I KNOW YOU CARE ABOUT YOUR BROTHER, SO YOU WON'T LIKE TO SEE HIM DEFEATED IN THE MOST HUMILIATING WAY POSSIBLE.
BUT UNFORTUNATELY FOR YAKO, YUGI HAS A SWORD. A SWORD I GAVE HIM.

A SWORD OF INCREDIBLE POWER!

I GAVE YOU A SWORD, YUGI! NOW USE IT AND SLAY THE EVIL GOD!
DO IT!!!
YES !!
THAT CARD IS ALREADY...
GET READY, YAKO!
BA
NG

FACE-DOWN SPELL CARD!
MONSTER REBORN!
MONSTER REBORN
(SPELL CARD)
Special Summon 1 monster from either player's Graveyard to your side of the field.
D-
D-
D-
D-
D-

GOD OF THE OBELISK!!!

COME FORTH!
THIS IS... YUGI'S GOD...
URGH...
DID HE SEND HIS GOD TO THE GRAVEYARD WHEN HE SUMMONED THE TRICKY...?
HMPH...
SO WHAT?

EVEN IF IT'S A GOD, MY EVIL GOD WILL TAKE ITS SHAPE!
LOOK WELL UPON THE ONE THAT SURPASSES YOUR "GOD"...
THE EVIL GOD OBELISK!!

OH NO...!
THE GOD OF THE OBELISK ATK 4000
THE EVIL GOD OBELISK ATK 4001
AGAINST THE POWER OF THE WICKED AVATAR, EVEN OBELISK THE TORMENTOR ISN'T ENOUGH!
HE SHOULD HAVE JUST LET THE GUARD TOKENS TAKE THE ATTACK...
MHEH HEH...
DON'T UNDERESTI-MATE OBELISK, GEKKO.
EVEN ON THE OPPONENT'S TURN, OBELISK CAN USE ITS ULTIMATE ABILITY TO ATTACK!

THE ULTIMATE POWER...
...OF THE GOD OF THE OBELISK!
I ACTIVATE OBELISK'S SPECIAL ABILITY...
INFINITE ATTACK POWER!
SOUL ENERGY MAX!!

BY OFFERING TWO SACRIFICES TO OBELISK, I RAISE HIS ATTACK POWER TO INFINITY!

YOU CAN'T ADD TO OR SUBTRACT FROM INFINITY! THAT MEANS AVATAR'S PLUS ONE IS USELESS!

INFINITY...

FOOL!

YOU CAN'T BEAT ME LIKE THAT!

THE JASHIN'S ATTACK POWER JUST ROSE TO INFINITY AS WELL!

G G G G

THE EVIL GOD OBELISK
ATK ∞

AND THAT'S NOT ALL! YOUR OBELISK AND MY EVIL GOD ARE OF DIFFERENT RANKS IN THE DIVINE HIERARCHY!

ANY ATTACK FROM A LOW-LEVEL GOD LIKE THAT...

...WILL BE NULL AND VOID!!

YA HA HA HA HA HA!
YUGI...

GEKKO.
!

I'M GOING...

...TO DEFEAT YOUR BROTHER.

THE CHAIN OF HATRED INSIDE YAKO...

...

THEN DO IT, YUGI.
IF IT'S YOU, I KNOW YOU'LL BE ABLE TO STOP HIM.

WHAT ARE YOU WAITING FOR? ATTACK, ATTACK, ATTACK!
SHATTER OBELISK!
YOU SAID OUR GODS' RANKS WERE DIFFERENT, DIDN'T YOU?
...
BUT THE DIVINE RANK OF OBELISK...
...HAS BEEN RAISED BY GEKKO, YOUR BROTHER!
BLAM

READ THIS WAY
I NOW ACTIVATE MY THIRD FACE-DOWN CARD!
BOOM
WHAT ...?!
THAT'S GEKKO'S CARD...!
BMP
SPELL CARD! DIVINE EVOLUTION! THANKS TO THIS CARD...
DIVINE EVOLUTION
(SPELL CARD)
The target monster gains 1000 ATK and DEF, for as long as it remains face-up on the field. This card's activation and effect cannot be negated by any other card.
...OBELISK THE TORMENTOR WILL ASCEND TO A HIGHER LEVEL...
G- G- G- G- G- G-

OBELISK THE PROGENITOR!!!

I... IMPOSSIBLE ...!!
THIS CAN'T BE... HOW DID HE...?
YAKO...
...
THIS IS IT!!!

OBELISK THE PRO-
GENITOR!
GOD HAND
IMPACT!!

KASHOOM
BLAM

GOD HAND!!
IMPACT !!!
THEY'RE GOING TO...!
NGH ...!
FLASH
DUEL ROUND 43: MUTUALLY ASSURED DESTRUCTION

Duel Round 43:
Mutually Assured Destruction

ZAP
ZAP
Z-ZAP
AGGGGH!
D
THIS... THIS ENERGY IS INSANE ...!
SKZZZT T T T
IS THE SERVER GOING TO HOLD UP?!
NGH...
ANZU!!
GZZT T T
!!

KRIK
OBELISK IS...
AVATAR IS... CRUMBLING!!
KA
CHOOM
RRGH...
!!

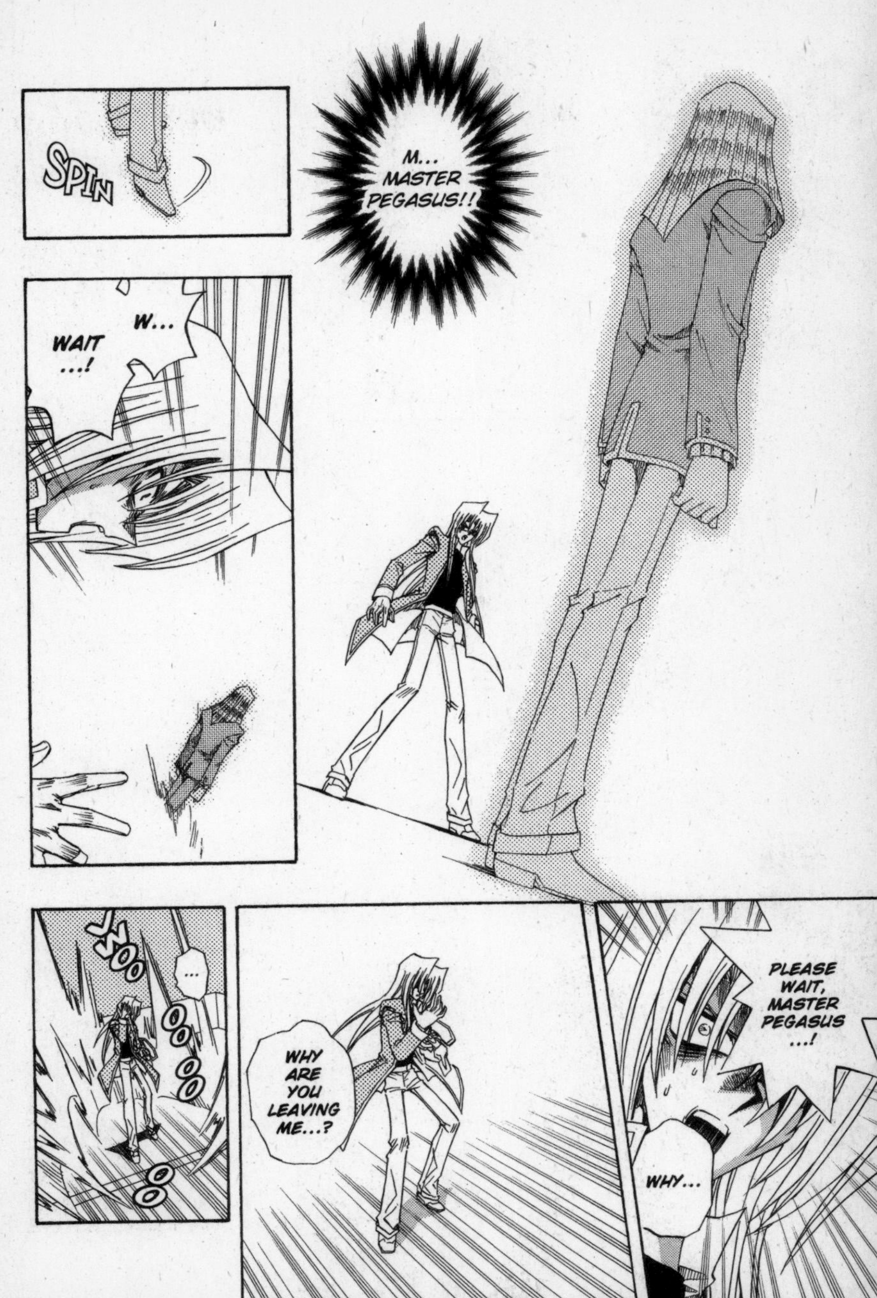
M... MASTER PEGASUS!!
SPIN
W... WAIT...!
PLEASE WAIT, MASTER PEGASUS...!
WHY...
WHY ARE YOU LEAVING ME...?
...

ANZU...
IT'S OKAY, YUGI...
I'LL BE BACK WITH YOU GUYS...
...BEFORE YOU KNOW IT...
I KNOW...
FWAA AA A

THE GOD...
THE EVIL GOD...

THEY'RE BOTH GONE ...!!

OH...

ANZU ?!
ARE YOU AWAKE?!

BOOM

...
BLINK
HONDA...
JONO-UCHI...

ALL RIGHT! YOU'RE ALIVE!

JUST HOLD ON! WE'LL GET YOU OUTTA THIS MACHINE RIGHT AWAY!
MAN... I'M SO HAPPY...

...
THANKS, YOU TWO...

NO...
DON'T THANK US YET...

YUGI'S STILL FIGHTING UP TOP!
WE'VE GOTTA GET UP THERE ASAP AND LET HIM KNOW YOU'RE OKAY!

RIGHT!

OKAY!
CAN YOU WALK, ANZU?
I THINK SO...

C'MON!
LET'S GO FIND YUGI!!

BIG BROTHER! THE DUEL RING SERVER HAS RETURNED TO NORMAL!

VERY GOOD.
BIP

I THOUGHT SO... SINCE THE WICKED AVATAR WAS DESTROYED ALONG WITH YUGI'S GOD...
...IT LOST ITS CONTROL OF THE DUEL RING SERVER!

AND I BET...
ITS INFLUENCE OVER YOUR BROTHER IS GONE AS WELL...

YAKO...

YAKO...

WE'VE BEEN FIGHTING ALL NIGHT. THE LIGHT OF A NEW DAY HAS SWALLOWED THE EVIL GOD JUST LIKE IT SWALLOWED THE DARKNESS.

IT'S TIME YOU LET GO.

...

YAKO. THE TWO GODS STRUCK AT EACH OTHER WITH MAXIMUM POWER. BOTH OF THEM WERE DESTROYED.
YAKO TENMA
Life Points 900
BUT THE TWO OF US ARE STILL ALIVE.
YUGI MUTOU
Life Points 98

HE'S GONE...

MASTER PEGASUS... IS GONE...
IT'S ALL... OVER...

MASTER PEGASUS... WENT INTO THE LIGHT...
HE JUST WENT AWAY... HE NEVER LOOKED BACK...

THERE'S... NO POINT...
...TO THIS FIGHT... NOT ANY-MORE...

HE'S GOING TO SURRENDER!

NO, YAKO!
YOU MUSTN'T END IT YET!

GEKKO... WH- WHY...?

B... BEFORE YOU STARTED THIS BATTLE...
...YOU TOLD ME THAT I WAS LIKE THE MOON... A REFLECTION OF PEGASUS.

YOU'RE RIGHT... WITHOUT THAT LIGHT...
...WITHOUT MASTER PEGASUS... I'M WORTHLESS.

...
BUT YAKO!
YOU'RE DIFFERENT!

EVEN ON THE DARKEST NIGHT, YOU CAN STILL KEEP GOING!

MASTER PEGASUS DIDN'T COMPLETE THE EVIL GOD CARDS...

...BECAUSE YOU WERE ALREADY STRONG ENOUGH WITHOUT THEM!

...!!

MASTER PEGASUS DIDN'T COME BACK TO US... HE WASN'T WAITING FOR US AT THE END OF THE BATTLE.

BUT...

YAKO! SOMEDAY, WHEN YOU'VE FOUGHT ENOUGH AND GROWN ENOUGH...

BAM

...YOU'LL FIND YOUR TRUE FORM, THE ONE MASTER PEGASUS SAW WITH HIS MILLENNIUM EYE!

AND THEN YOU WON'T NEED THE EVIL GODS OR ANYTHING LIKE THEM!

CLENCH

YUGI... I...
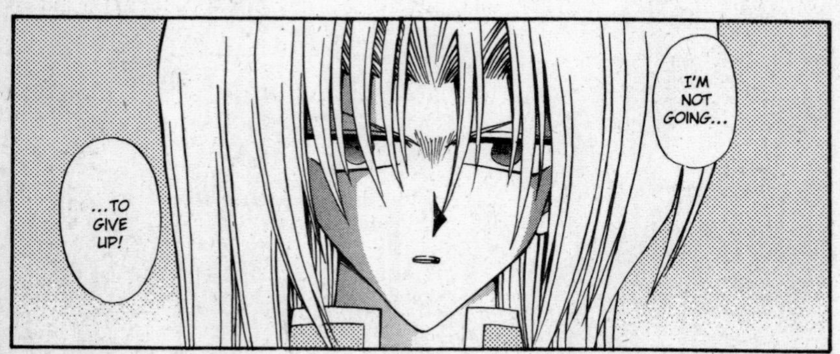
I'M NOT GOING...
...TO GIVE UP!

YAKO!!

HEH ...

FINE!
THEN FIGHT ME!

THE EVIL GOD WAS DEFEATED...
...BUT MY TURN HASN'T ENDED YET!

FROM MY HAND, I ACTIVATE...

...THE SPELL CARD ***LEVEL AWARD!***

WITH THIS CARD...

...I RAISE ***METAL FIEND TOKEN'S*** LEVEL TO EIGHT!

LEVEL AWARD

(SPELL CARD)

Change the Level of 1 monster on the field to any number of your choice between 0 and 8.

METAL FIEND
★★★★★
★★★

WHY IS IT...?

NOW... I CAN HEAR GEKKO'S VOICE SO CLEARLY...

"YOUR TRUE FORM, THE ONE MASTER PEGASUS SAW WITH HIS MILLENNIUM EYE...!"

...
MY TRUE FORM... I WONDER WHAT THAT COULD BE...?

YUGI MUTOU!

GEKKO! DID YOU REALLY MEAN WHAT YOU SAID...?
ALSO...

TO KNOW THE ANSWER... I HAVE TO BEAT YOU!
REVERSE CARD, OPEN!
STAR LEVEL SHUFFLE!
BA
NG

I REPLACE THE NEW EIGHT-STAR METAL FIEND WITH AN EIGHT-STAR MONSTER FROM MY GRAVEYARD!
STAR LEVEL SHUFFLE
(SPELL CARD)
Send 1 monster you control to your Graveyard to Special Summon 1 monster from your Graveyard with the same Level as the monster you sent to the Graveyard.
FROM THE GRAVE I CALL FORTH...
THE EIGHT-STAR BEAST KING BARBAROS!!

BARBAROS ...!!

SINCE I SPECIAL SUMMONED HIM FROM THE GRAVEYARD, BARBAROS ISN'T WEAK LIKE HE WAS LAST TIME!

THIS IS BARBAROS'S TRUE FORM!
HIS ATTACK POWER IS 3000!!
BEAST KING BARBAROS
You can Normal Summon or Set this card without Tributing. If you do, its original ATK becomes 1900. You can Tribute 3 monsters to Tribute Summon this card. When you do, destroy all cards your opponent controls.
ATK 3000 DEF 1200

SO THIS IS YAKO...

LEVEL TRICK TACTICS, HUH...
HE MAY NOT BE POSSESSED BY THE EVIL GODS ANYMORE, BUT IT LOOKS LIKE HE'S STILL A STRONG DUELIST!

YAKO ...

THAT ENDS MY TURN.

ZM

ZM

ZM

ZM

YAKO...
THIS DUEL ISN'T THE SAME AS BEFORE.

NOW THAT YOU'VE LOST THE EVIL GODS...
...THIS ISN'T A GRUDGE MATCH ANYMORE...
IT ISN'T ABOUT WRATH OR REVENGE...

THIS...

...IS A BATTLE BETWEEN DUELISTS!

SHOW ME HOW YOU REALLY FIGHT...!

HERE I GO!!

IT'S MY TURN!

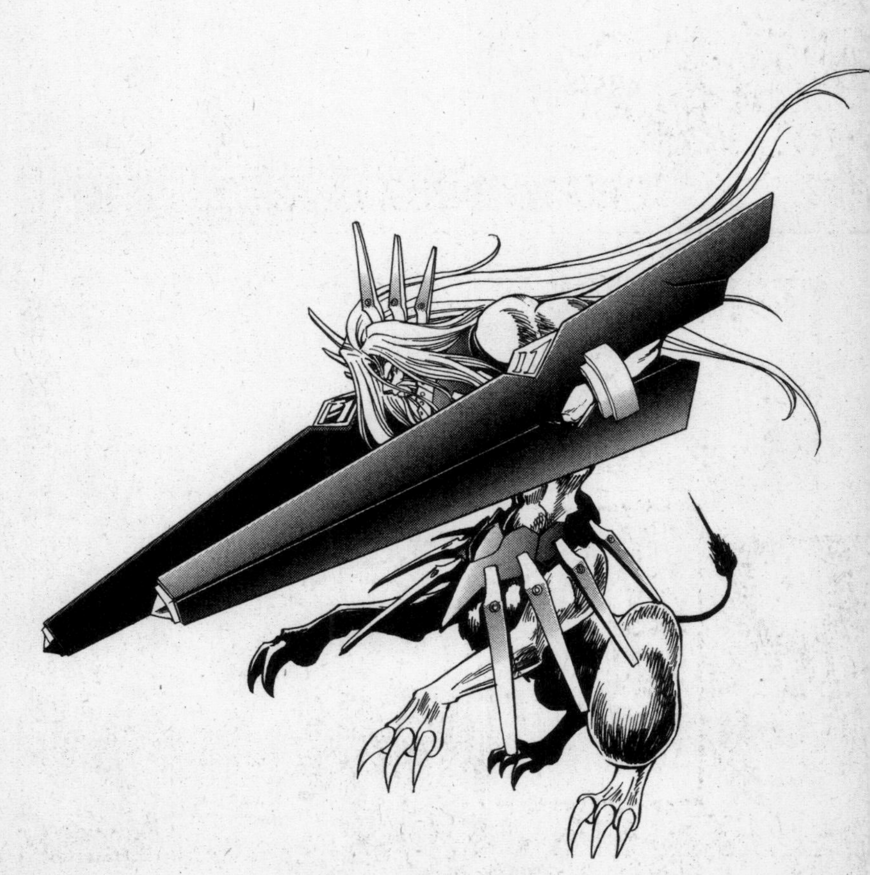

Duel Round 44: The End of the Battle

NEITHER OF US CAN HOPE FOR A SATISFYING DUEL WITH THE HANDS WE HAVE NOW.

I PLAY THE SPELL CARD, *CARD OF SANCTITY!*
CARD OF SANCTITY
(SPELL CARD)
Both players draw cards until each player has 6 cards in his hand.
HUH ...?
B-BMP
BANG

WE'LL EACH DRAW UNTIL WE BOTH HAVE SIX CARDS IN OUR HAND!

HUH? EVEN THOUGH YAKO ALREADY HAS BARBAROS, WITH ITS 3000 ATTACK POINTS...

YUGI STILL...

I SET ONE CARD FACE DOWN!

BAM

THEN I SUMMON BETA THE MAGNET WARRIOR IN DEFENSE MODE!

TURN OVER!

ALL RIGHT. COME AT ME...
...WITH EVERYTHING YOU'VE GOT!!

MY TURN...

...

ZM
ZM
ZM
ZM

WHAT'S WRONG WITH YAKO? HE'S ACTING STRANGE...
MHEH HEH...

HE THOUGHT HIS EVIL GOD WAS INVINCIBLE, BUT HE LOST IT TO THREE FACE-DOWN CARDS!
LOOK! YUGI HAS ONE CARD FACE DOWN ON HIS FIELD...

THAT SINGLE CARD...
...IS MAKING YAKO HESITATE TO ATTACK!

YAKO...

RGH...

BARBAROS ...

ATTACK BETA THE MAGNET WARRIOR!!
!!
TORNADO SHAPER!!
HUH...
GOOD!
IT SEEMS YOUR DUELIST'S SOUL IS STILL ALIVE!

BETA THE MAGNET WARRIOR FADED OUT...?!

SWISH

BAM

AH! HE USED A RELIEF ESCAPE TO DODGE THE ATTACK!

SOUL BARTER
(SPELL CARD)

Select 1 monster in your Graveyard. Send 1 face-up monster on your side of the field to the Graveyard to Special Summon the selected monster. The summoned monster must be placed in the same Battle Position as the monster that was sent to the Graveyard by this effect.

BAM

USING THE EFFECT OF SOUL BARTER, I SUMMON ALPHA THE MAGNET WARRIOR FROM THE GRAVEYARD!!

I...SET ONE CARD FACE DOWN.
THAT ENDS MY TURN.
BAM
...
MY TURN.

I PUT ONE FACE-DOWN CARD ON THE FIELD.
BAM
THEN I SUMMON BLOCKMAN IN DEFENSE MODE!!
BLOCKMAN
ATK 1000 DEF 1500
DOM

TURN OVER!
IT'S ALL YUGI CAN DO TO GET DEFENSE MONSTERS IN PLACE.
AND BARBAROS IS STRONG, BUT YAKO'S HAVING TROUBLE ATTACKING...

WATCH CLOSELY! THE TIDE OF THIS BATTLE IS ABOUT TO TURN!
MY TURN...
ANY MOMENT NOW...!
HERE I COME...
I SUMMON "MACHINE LORD ÜR"!!
MACHINE LORD ÜR
This card can attack all monsters your opponent controls once each. Any Battle Damage this card inflicts to your opponent becomes 0.
ATK/1600 DEF/1500
BAM
DOOM
THEN I ACTIVATE A SPELL CARD FROM MY HAND!

GWOOOOO
!!
I FUSE BEAST KING BARBAROS AND MACHINE LORD ÜR!
POLYMERIZATION
(SPELL CARD)
POLYMER-IZATION!
BEAST MACHINE KING...
...BARBAROS ÜR!!!
BEAST MACHINE KING BARBAROS ÜR
ATK 3800

BARBAROS ÜR IS ALMOST A GOD...

...AND IT HAS INHERITED MACHINE KING ÜR'S SPECIAL ABILITY!

D D D D D

!!

MACHINE KING ÜR'S ABILITY...

IN OTHER WORDS...

IT CAN ATTACK A NUMBER OF OPPONENTS EQUAL TO ITS STAR LEVEL!

SINCE BARBAROS ÜR IS AN EIGHT-STAR MONSTER, IT CAN TAKE OUT BOTH OF YOUR DEFENSE MONSTERS AT ONCE!!

BAM

FURTHER-MORE, I ACTIVATE MY FACE-DOWN CARD, QUICK ATTACK!

QUICK ATTACK
(SPELL CARD)
Select 1 Fusion Monster you Fusion Summoned this turn. That Fusion Monster may attack this turn.

THIS CARD ALLOWS MY FUSION MONSTER TO ATTACK ON THIS TURN!!

KA'CHIK
BEAST MACHINE KING BARBAROS ÜR ATTACKS!!
FLASHBURST SHOT!!!

REVERSE CARD, OPEN!
NEGATE ATTACK!
NEGATE ATTACK
(SPELL CARD)
Activate only when an opponent's monster declares an attack. Negate the attack and end the Battle Phase.
WHROOSHHH
...
I CAN'T CHIP AWAY AT HIM...

HE HAS ONLY... ONLY 98 LIFE POINTS LEFT...
BUT HE MIGHT AS WELL HAVE 98,000...

...

MY TURN!
I REALIZE NOW...

EVEN WITH AN OVERWHELMINGLY POWERFUL MONSTER, A DEMIGOD, ON MY SIDE...
...HE'S TOO HIGH ABOVE ME...

WHOOOSH

I SACRIFICE ALPHA THE MAGNET WARRIOR...

DARK MAGICIAN GIRL

ATK 2000 DEF 1700

DA

...AND SUMMON THE *DARK MAGICIAN GIRL!!*

KA

THIS IS IT! HE'S CROSSING OVER...

...MY WALL OF MONSTERS!

YAKO...
HERE I COME!!
I ACTIVATE BLOCKMAN'S SPECIAL ABILITY!!
KLAK
KLAK
IT SPLITS INTO TWO BLOCK MONSTERS!
I ACTIVATE A SPELL CARD FROM MY HAND!!
MAGICAL DIMENSION!!
MAGICAL DIMENSION
(SPELL CARD)
Activate only while you control a Spellcaster-Type monster. Tribute 2 monsters and Special Summon 1 Spellcaster-Type monster from your hand. Then, you can destroy 1 monster on the field.
VOOM
THIS IS...
I SACRIFICE THE TWO BLOCK MONSTERS...
COME FORTH!
BAM

KREEK
THE ULTIMATE WIZARD, THE DARK MAGICIAN !!!
TSK TSK!
THE DARK MAGICIAN AND HIS APPRENTICE WILL FIGHT TOGETHER..
...AND DESTROY ONE MONSTER !!

VREEEEEN
BLAM
MMMMM
BLACK BURNING MAGIC!!

BARBAROS ÜR WAS DEFEATED ...
MHEH HEH HEH... NOT BAD...
WOW...
YAKO...
YOU WERE A MIGHTY OPPONENT!

YUGI...
AND NOW, FOR THE LAST ACTION OF MY TURN!
THE DARK MAGICIAN GIRL ATTACKS!
ZWOOSH
BLACK BURNING !!

YUGI'S POWER...

...IS MAGNIFICENT...

HWOOOOO

YAKO TENMA
Life Points 0

IT'S OVER!

BAM

KAIBA!

YOU RESCUED THE KAIBACORP SKYSCRAPER FROM THESE INVADERS.
FOR THAT, I THANK YOU.

YAKO...

THANK YOU FOR MAKING ME FINISH THE DUEL.
IF I'D LET IT END THAT WAY, I WOULD HAVE REGRETTED IT.

I'LL ALWAYS WISH WE STILL HAD MASTER PEGASUS...

...BUT I HAVE TO CUT THE CORD.
RIP
RIP

YUGI!!

GUYS!

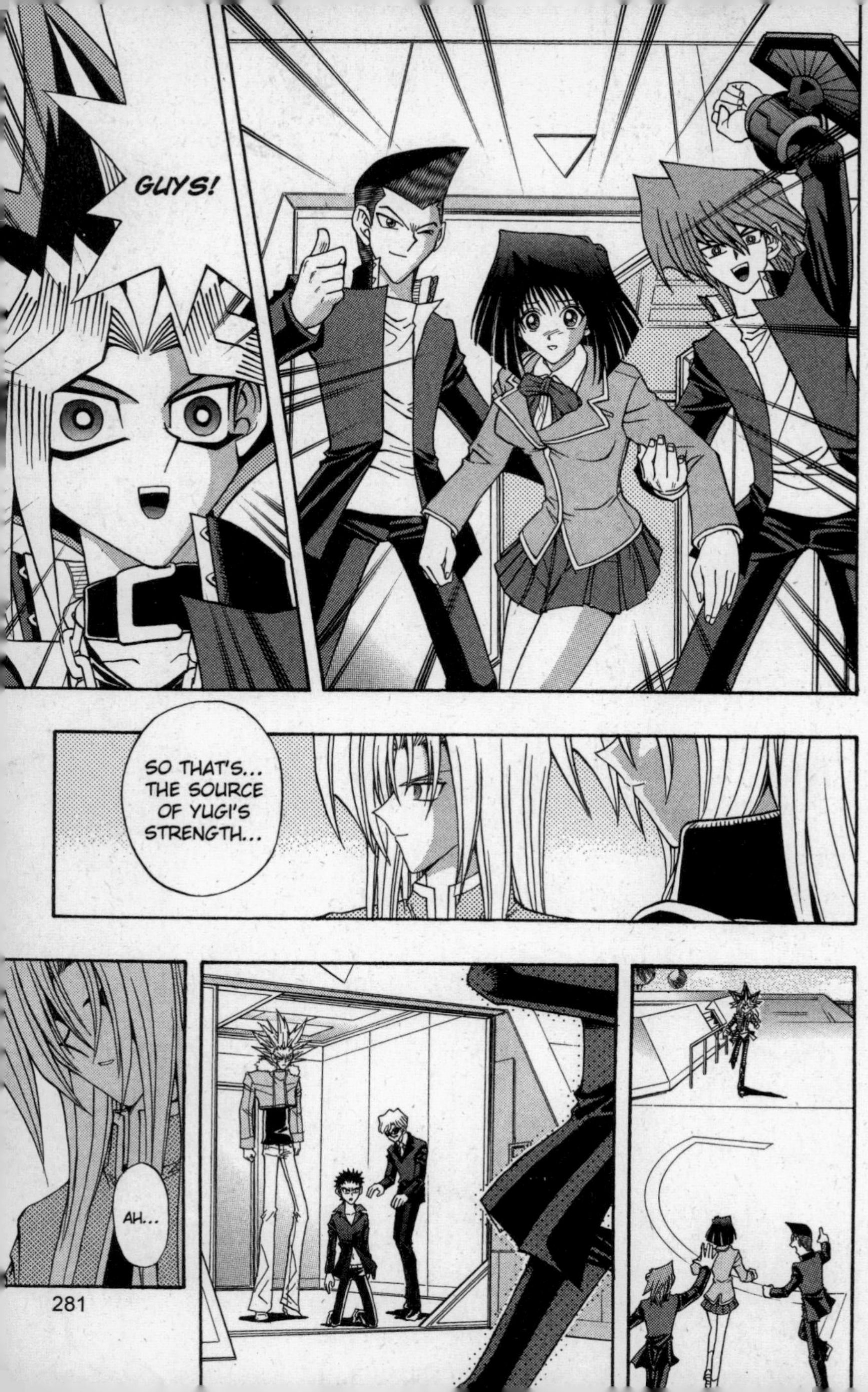

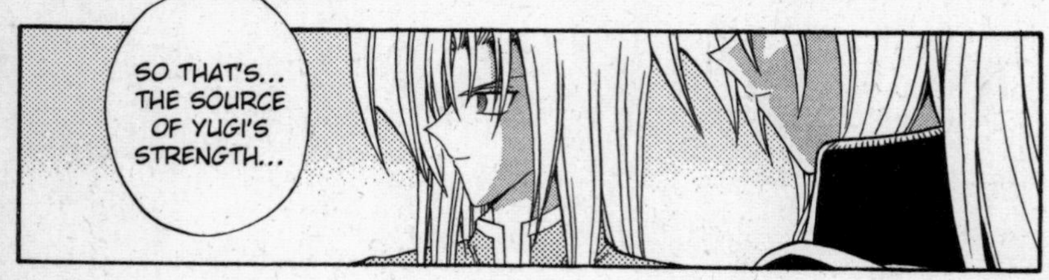

SO THAT'S... THE SOURCE OF YUGI'S STRENGTH...

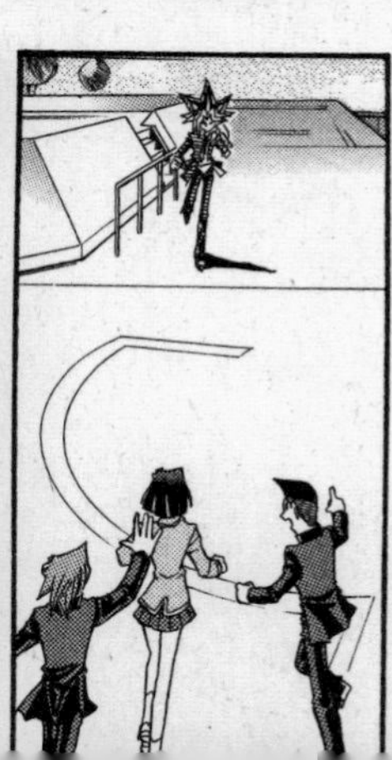

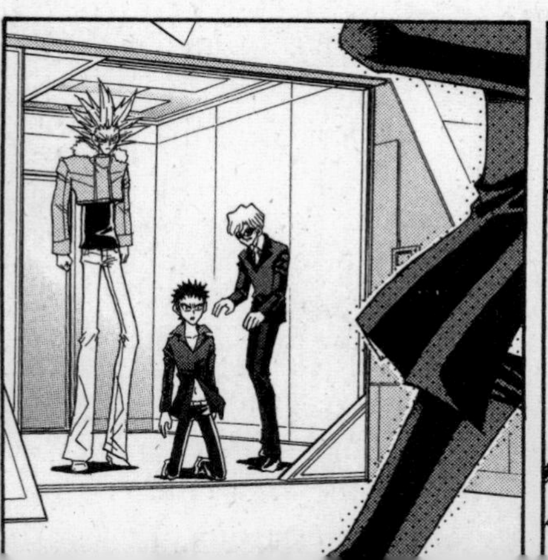

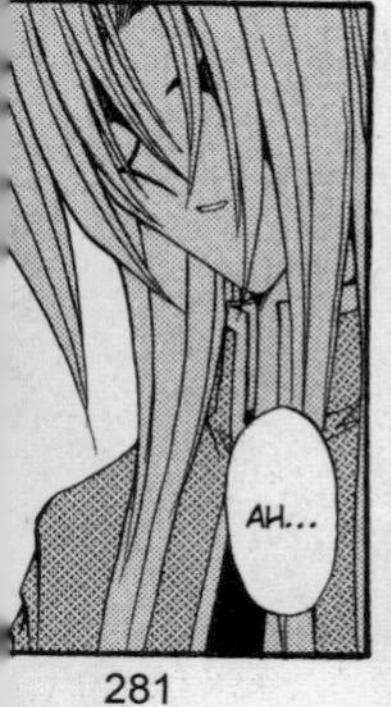

AH...

OH!
WOBBLE
I'M GLAD I DIDN'T ERASE...
...THOSE SMILES...

Original Concept
Kazuki Takahashi

Art
Akira Ito

Staff
Naoyuki Kageyama
Akihiro Tomonaga
Masafumi Sato
Makoto Shimizu
Ryuji Goto
Daiji Fukuzawa
Keiichi Hayashi
Chikahide Makioka

Cooperation
Wedge Holdings Co., Ltd.
Naoto Okawa
Tatsuyuki Sugawara
Masahiro Uchida
Tetsuya Hoshi
Toru Inoue

Editing
Daisuke Terashi

KC
KC
KC
KC
YU-GI-OH! R: THE END

TER OF THE CARDS

I TAKAHASHI. Manufactured and distributed by Konami Digital Entertainment, c. KONAMI is a registered trademark of KONAMI CORPORATION.

al story that takes place after *Yu-Gi-Oh!: Duelist* but before *World*. It features many new cards never seen before in the th all original *Yu-Gi-Oh!* cards, names can differ slightly between ish versions, so we're showing you both for reference. Plus, even if the card itself doesn't show up in the manga but the And some cards you may have already seen in the original ote them the first time they appear in this volume anyway!

THIS VOLUME

Japanese Card Name	English Card Name <<!>> = Not yet available in the TCG.
Little-Winguard リトル・ウィンガード	Little-Winguard
Motor Shell モーターシェル	Motor Shell <<!>>
Shikkoku no Hyôsenshi Panther Warrior 漆黒の彪戦士パンサー・ウォリアー	Panther Warrior
Engine Tuner エンジンチューナー	Engine Tuner <<!>>
Monster Box モンスターBOX	Fairy Box
Saint Knight Ishzark セイントナイトイシュザーク	Divine Knight Ishzark
Motor Parts モーターパーツ	Motor Parts <<!>>
Motor Violence モーターバイオレンス	Motor Violence <<!>>
Toki no Kikai Time Machine 時の機械－タイム・マシーンー	Time Machine
Gilford the Lightning ギルフォード・ザ・ライトニング	Gilford the Lightning
Take Over テイク・オーバー	Take Over <<!>>

p.36	*Hakairin* 破壊輪	Ring of Destruction
p.38	*Toki no Majutsushi* 時の魔術師	Time Wizard
p.38	*Kakuritsu Hendô* 確率変動	Probability Change <<!>>
p.41	*Motor Kaiser* モーター・カイザル	Motor Kaiser <<!>>
p.43	*Card Hexative* カード・ヘキサチーブ	Card Hexative <<!>>
p.45	*Scrap Garage* スクラップ・ガレージ	Scrap Garage <<!>>
p.48	*The Devils Eraser*	The Wicked Eraser
p.58	*Hurricane* ハリケーン	Giant Trunade
p.59	*Mahô Kaijo* 魔法解除	De-Spell
p.67	*Haka Arashi* 墓荒し	Graverobber
p.69	*Summon Capture* サモン・キャプチャー	Summon Capture <<!>>
p.71	*Demonic Motor Omega* デモニック・モーターオメガ	Fiendish Engine Ω
p.83	*Nikoichi* ニコイチ	Two-for-One Repair Job <<!>>
p.84	*Akuma no Saikoro* 悪魔のサイコロ	Skull Dice
p.89	*Tetsu no Kishi Gear Fried* 鉄の騎士ギア・フリード	Gearfried the Iron Knight
p.124	*Magnet Warrior Alpha* マグネット・ウォリアー アルファ	Alpha the Magnet Warrior
p.125	*Shinjûô Barbaros* 神獣王バルバロス	Beast King Barbaros
p.127	*Tamashii no Tsuna* 魂の綱	Soul Rope
p.128	*Kings Knight* キングス・ナイト	King's Knight
p.128	*Queens Knight* クィーンズ・ナイト	Queen's Knight

p.129	*Jacks Knight* ジャックス・ナイト	Jack's Knight
p.131	*Yûgo* 融合	Polymerization
p.132	*Arcana Knight Joker* アルカナ・ナイト・ジョーカー	Arcana Knight Joker
p.134	*Level Resist Wall* レベル・レジストウォール	Level Resist Wall <<!>>
p.134	*Angel 01* エンジェル０１	Angel 01 <<!>>
p.134	*Cassimolar* カシモラル	Cassimolar <<!>>
p.134	*Leraje the God of Archery* 弓神レライエ	Leraje the God of Archery <<!>>
p.135	*Votis* ボティス	Votis <<!>>
p.150	*Big Shield Gardna* ビッグ・シールド・ガードナー	Big Shield Gardna
p.154	*Gunshin Gaap* 軍神ガープ	Gaap the Divine Soldier
p.156	*The Devils Avatar*	The Wicked Avatar
p.159	*Cross Counter Trap* クロス・カウンター・トラップ	Cross Counter Trap <<!>>
p.159	*Meifu nisshuke Kaidan* 冥府につつく階段	Stairway to the Underworld <<!>>
p.160	*Meifu no Shisha Gorz* 冥府の使者コーソ	Gorz the Emissary of Darkness
p.160	*Meifu no Shisha Kaien* 冥府の使者カイエン	Kaien the Emissary of Darkness <<!>>
p.164	*Teki Shûkeihô—Yellow Alert* 敵襲警報ーイエローアラートー	Yellow Alert <<!>>
p.165	*Shôtenshi Tellus* 小天使テルス	Tellus the Little Angel <<!>>

p.165	*Tellus no Hane* テルスの羽	Tellus' Wing <<!>>
p.166	*Zôshoku* 増殖	Multiply
p.182	*The Tricky* THEトリッキー	The Tricky
p.183	*Union Attack* ユニオン・アタック	Union Attack
p.186	*Chikara no Shôshitsu* 力の消失	Loss of Strength <<!>>
p.188	*Devil's Sanctuary* デビルズ・サンクチュアリ	Fiend's Sanctuary
p.188	*Metal Devil Token* メタルデビル・トークン	Metal Fiend Token
p.196	*Hikari no Gofûken* 光の護封剣	Swords of Revealing Light
p.198	*Monster Kaishû* モンスター回収	Monster Recovery
p.217	*Shadow Guardsmen* シャドーガードマン	Shadow Guardsmen <<!>>
p.217	*Eihei Token* 衛兵トークン	Guard Token <<!>>
p.218	*Berserk Mode* バーサーク・モード	Berserk Mode
p.221	*Shisha Sosei* 死者蘇生	Monster Reborn
p.221	*The God of Obelisk*	The God of the Obelisk
p.231	*Kami no Shinka* 神の進化	Divine Evolution <<!>>
p.254	*Level Award* レベル・アワード	Level Award <<!>>
p.255	*Star Level Shuffle* スターレベル・シャッフル	Star Level Shuffle <<!>>
p.261	*Ten yori no Hôsatsu* 天よりの宝札	Card of Sanctity <<!>>
p.262	*Magnet Warrior Beta* マグネット・ ウォリアーベータ	Beta the Magnet Warrior
p.265	*Tamashii no Kôkan—Soul Barter* 魂の交換ーソウル・バーター	Soul Barter <<!>>

p.266	*Blockman* ブロックマン	Blockman
p.267	*Shinkiô Ur* 神機王ウル	Machine Lord Ür
p.269	*Sokkô* 速攻	Quick Attack <<!>>
p.271	*Kôgeki no Muryokuka* 攻撃の無力化	Negate Attack
p.273	*Black Magician Girl* ブラック・マジシャンガール	Dark Magician Girl
p.274	*Dimension Magic* ディメンション・マジック	Magical Dimension
p.275	*Black Magician* ブラック・マジシャン	Dark Magician

R0452973821

Pig and Twig
are playing princess.
"I'll be the princess," says Pig.
"Make three wishes," says Twig.

“I wish for lipstick!”
says Princess Pig.
“Swish! Wish!” says Twig.

"I wish for a picnic!"
says Princess Pig.
"Swish! Wish!" says Twig.

"I wish for kittens—
in mittens!"
says Princess Pig.
"Swish! Wish!"
says Twig.

"Now I will be the princess," says Twig.
"Not yet," says Princess Pig.
"I wish to make more wishes."

"I wish for nickels!"
says Princess Pig.
"Swish! Wish!" says Twig.

"I wish for pickles!"
says Princess Pig.
"Swish! Wish!" says Twig.

FRIGIDAIRE

"I wish for sixteen pink popsicles!"
says Princess Pig.
"Swish! Wish!" says Twig.

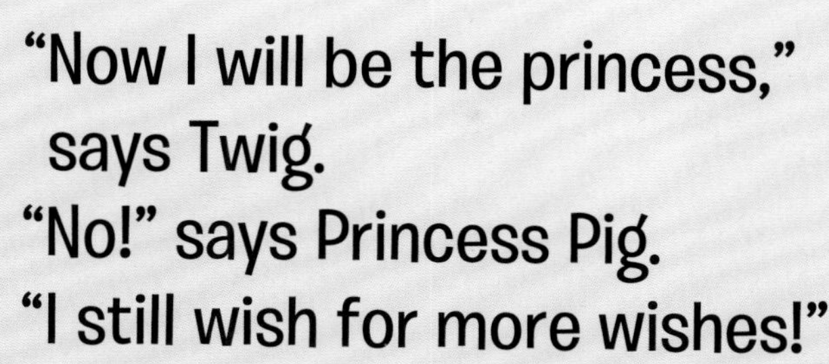

"Now I will be the princess,"
says Twig.
"No!" says Princess Pig.
"I still wish for more wishes!"

"No more wishes," says Twig.
"I quit!"

Pig misses Twig.

"Will you be the princess now?" asks Pig.
"Yippee!" says Twig.
"Make three wishes," says Pig.

“I wish to skip,

and sip,

and take a dip,
with my friend Pig!"

The End

Story Starters

Pig gives Twig another wish.
What will Twig wish?

Pig says,
“Swish! Wish! Make a wish!”
What will you wish?

Twig has a gift for Sis.
What is it?